KIDS 'n' CASH

How to raise money-wise children

by Judith A. Schmatjen

Tzedakah Publications
Sacramento, California

For information, address
Tzedakah Publications
P.O. Box 221097
Sacramento, CA 95822
1-800-316-1824

Cover and Page Design: Comstock's Design & Litho (Mary Burroughs
and Jill Raymond)
Cover Illustration: Diane Sutherland Art Direction

Library of Congress Cataloging-in-Publication Data
Schmatjen, Judith A.
Kids 'n' cash: how to raise money-wise children / by Judith A. Schmatjen. --
First Edition
ISBN 0-929999-08-8, $9.95
1. Saving and thrift--United States. 2. Children--United States-Finance-Personal.
3. Children's allowances--United States. 4. Child rearing--United States. I. Title.
HQ784.S4S33 1995   94-47433
649'.1--dc20   CIP

10 9 8 7 6 5 4 3 2 1

None of the information in this publication should be construed as professional
financial advice. If expert investment or financial assistance is needed, please
consult a professional investment or financial firm.

Table of Contents

This book is dedicated to my husband, Dave, whose wisdom, patience, and sense of humor always keep me on track.

Acknowledgments

Whether talking to close friends or complete strangers, I learned that "kids and money" is a high-energy subject. I'm grateful to all those people who shared their stories with me, particularly those friends who read my first manuscript and broadened my horizons: Linda Book, Flo Grossenbacher, Marylee Hardie, Leigh Hyde, Mimi Legakis, Peggy Phister, Paula Rehwaldt, and Mary Lou Rossetto. I'm especially beholden to my husband, Dave, and children, Jill Arena, Heidi Schmatjen, and Marc Schmatjen, who gave me abundant feedback and always cheered me on.

And thanks to my editor, Michael Gorman, who was wonderful to work with. His talent for fine-tuning words and making ideas come alive is impressive. John Swanson and Jill Arena also have my great appreciation for making me computer literate, even on days when I didn't want to be.

Finally, I would like to thank the entire staff at Tzedakah Publications for their guidance, especially David Cawthorn, who urged me to expand my ideas and write this book.

*"Don't give your children
the trappings of success.
Give them the tools
to make their own successes."*

David L. Schmatjen, Dad

Introduction

It's probably the most important job a person can do.
It is certainly one of the most difficult. Yet it requires no
license, no degree, and no bar examination. There is no
on-the-job training, and no one can agree on an instruction manual. The possible pitfalls are so numerous, it's a
wonder any of us ever successfully do it at all. I refer, of
course, to raising children.

For some reason, the responsibility of parenting didn't
hit me until I was cradling our firstborn child in my arms.
I felt such love for that innocent, vulnerable little person.
Seconds later, the magnitude of the job hit full force. Our
daughter barely weighed six pounds, but the weight on
my shoulders felt like six tons. I looked at my husband and
blurted out, "WE HAVE TO TAKE CARE OF HER!"

Soon the initial shock of having a child wore off, and
we adjusted to parenthood pretty well. Our family eventually grew to three children, and, like most parents, we
figured the job out day by day and made it through quite
nicely. This year our last child graduated from college,
and we marked twenty-five years of parenting.

During those years of raising our children, my husband and I tried to teach them the skills they would need
to live happily and prosperously on their own. One of
those important life skills was the handling of money. Out
of necessity (the mother of invention), we developed a
system designed to teach our kids good money management and a realistic attitude toward money.

Like most parents, we told our success stories to
other parents as a way of passing on what we had
learned. The idea of sharing our methods by writing a
book, however, did not happen until our children hit the
junior high level. A teacher friend knew we had a plan
regarding our kids and money, and she invited us to
attend a PTA-sponsored seminar on "Teens and Money."

That evening we found out that money and teens was a hot topic. We were barraged with questions.

Months later, parents were still coming up to us saying, "I remember when you shared your allowance system at Emerson Junior High. I really liked your ideas." I was cornered in the grocery store, on the tennis court, in the bank, and at church by parents who wanted more information.

The information we shared at the junior high seminar that night was just one step in our system to teach our children responsibility and realism about money. (We had actually started some simple lessons about money around kindergarten.) After discovering how difficult this issue is for so many parents, we found ourselves wanting, more than ever, to share what we had learned.

There is such a temptation to ignore money when raising children, or to sit them down once and say, "This is how to be a responsible money manager . . . " and be done with it. But, as we all know, learning takes time and patience and guidance. Ignoring the problem will make it worse in the future. A child who doesn't develop good money habits while growing up may end up back on your doorstep at age twenty with an empty wallet and no plans for the future.

You can avoid such a scenario by teaching good money habits early. It can make your life and their life a lot easier. Our children are handling their financial affairs well, and yours can too. That is why I am writing this book, one parent to another.

The chapters are divided into age groups so that you can concentrate on the particular needs of your child's age, but I recommend that you read the entire plan so that you can keep each age in perspective, and so you will be prepared for your next step.

I have included quite a few stories about kids and money, because that is the true test of the value of this system: how it relates to the children. This plan is not some academic theory. It was worked out in the real world of real kids.

For quick reference, I have included charts for each age group. The charts summarize the material in the chapter and remind you of the focus at each age. Certainly, read the whole book, but also make it work for you as a handy reference guide.

I may not be able to meet with you over the back fence to answer your questions or share your victories as I have done with some of my neighbors, but I hope that through these pages I will be able to be there with you anyway as questions arise. Sometimes, in this difficult task of parenting, we are each other's most valuable resource.

Chapter 1

You're in Charge

A successful allowance system begins with you. We parents are, after all, in charge of the family finances. Once we accept our responsibility in the realm of money, we can set our expectations for our children and start the process of teaching them money matters through an allowance.

That all sounds simple enough until you hear from someone like my neighbor Karen. She applauded my desire to teach my kids about money but said that it's not that simple. She explained her bewilderment at the way her ten-year-old twins, Sarah and Michael, handle money.

Sarah zooms by on her new roller blades, while Michael tries to catch up on his old roller skates with the wobbly wheels. Karen shakes her head as she watches him struggle and then turns to me to talk. "Sarah saved her allowance for weeks to buy those roller blades," she sighs. "Michael tried to save up too, but whenever he got a little bit saved he blew it on cheap squirt guns and other plastic toys that broke. Sarah always has money for dolls and little gifts for family birthdays. She even puts a little money in the collection plate at church. I don't know what I did different with Michael. He can't even get through the week managing his lunch money. He's so careless with it. Sometimes he doesn't even know where he put it."

After talking to Karen, you might wonder if an allowance system will work at all. What if your children are like Michael? Will your efforts be wasted? And what if they are like Sarah? Won't they figure it out on their own?

The truth is that both Sarah and Michael needed guidance, but they were not on the same wavelength or at the same maturity level when it came to money. That's okay. You will have to respect your children's differences and provide individual support and encouragement along the way. A child like Michael just needs a little more time and guidance in money matters. Perhaps money may never be as high a priority for him as it is for Sarah, but that too is okay. Don't expect the same results from each child.

Money Is Not the Root of All Evil

Some of you may look at your own finances and wonder how you can possibly teach your children about money. Take heart. Now that you've decided to accept being in charge, there's some good news. You can teach your children about money in a positive and enjoyable manner even if your own money skills are not the best. Sometimes the most effective way to learn is by teaching. With this plan already worked out and "field tested" for you, teaching your children about money doesn't have to cause you aggravation.

It's easiest, of course, to start early, using the allowance as a hands-on tool that teaches sharing, saving, and budgeting, but it is never too late to start teaching money management skills to your child. If your children are older and the tug-of-war over money has already begun, there is no better time to launch the system. By doing so, you can avoid the arguments over money, and you can rid yourself of the guilt about what you do and don't buy your children.

In order to make the system work from the beginning, you will have to forget those taboos that say money is evil and not something you should ever talk about. We tend to be uncomfortable with money precisely because we don't talk about it. Take the time to talk to your children about your plan for their finances so that you can both relax about it.

This could lead to deeper discussions of your own finances as a way of providing a role model, but that is not necessary and should only be shared at your own discretion. By talking about finance, even if it is limited to the specifics of the allowance plan, you'll be laying the foundation for your children to have a happy relationship with money.

Few of us would hand the car keys over to our sixteen-year-olds and let them drive away without first having some driver training. In the same manner, it's important to take charge and train your children to handle money before they leave your nest. This can be done gradually and lovingly during their childhood years.

With a set plan, you can be in control and you can make it a positive and enjoyable endeavor — even through the teenage years.

¢ *Put yourself in charge of the family finances*

¢ *Know that each child will handle allowance money differently*

¢ *Talk about money — it shouldn't be a taboo subject*

Chapter 2

An Overview of the Plan

Now that we've established that an allowance plan can be a real benefit to you and your children, and that you can teach such a plan, whatever your own past financial history reveals, we need to take a quick look at the overall plan so you know what you're getting yourself into. I will discuss each part of the plan in detail in later chapters, but this overview will give you a foundation for setting some of your initial expectations. You can also use this chapter later as a quick refresher and reminder of the overall scope of the plan. It helps to keep each age level in perspective.

This allowance system begins at age five and continues until your child is a financially independent adult in his early twenties. It begins with a small allowance and no financial responsibilities beyond learning the basic function of money: that it buys things. As the plan progresses, the money increases along with the financial responsibility. The plan also includes guidelines for the transition into college. It is set up by age group, as follows:

Age 5: Money + Guidance

Ages 6-8: Money + Guidance + Financial Responsibility

Ages 9-11: Money + Guidance + More Financial Responsibility

> ### Ages 12-17: Money + Minimal Guidance +
> ### Lots of Financial Responsibility
>
> ### Ages 18-22: Some or No Money + No Guidance
> ### (Unless They Ask) + All of the Financial Responsibility

You will find this system especially helpful as your children reach junior high school age. At this time, they begin to see and understand "status symbols." Their desire for more money and material things increases dramatically. How do you explain to your child that your money supply has limits, and your paychecks stretch only so far? This system can be your answer because it guides you through the trouble spots.

Different Strokes for Different Young Folks

The age divisions I've used to organize the plan are not etched in stone. They are simply guidelines, approximations. They reflect my experience with my own children. Always let your own child's maturity level be your guide. Feel free to adjust the cutoff times to fit your child.

Children also differ a great deal in personality. This plan won't change a child's basic individuality, but different personalities can benefit from it. Maybe you have a spendthrift who goes through money as fast as he gets it and is always asking for more to solve his constant cash crisis. Maybe you have a child who clutches her every dollar and won't share any of it. Perhaps your child worries about keeping up with his lavish-spending friends. You might have an older child concerned about paying for her college education.

Being on an allowance system can ease these concerns and tendencies. A few months on this system can help a spendthrift know how to monitor his spending. He will know when the next allowance is paid and be forced to budget until then. The child who clutches her money may learn to share because she is assured of a regular allowance to replace the money spent or given away. With increased skill in money management, worriers gain confidence, and with advice on saving money, the college-bound student can start her education with money ahead.

Personality differences are clearly evident in the twins, Sarah and Michael, described in Chapter 1. They are very much alike in some respects and worlds apart in the area of handling money. Their mom, Karen, just needs to respect their differences and provide encouragement and support along the way. Michael's money slips through his hands, so he needs to get his allowance divided into smaller amounts that are paid more often to help him budget. He needs a specific place to keep his money (a jar or a bank will do) and instructions for saving. He also needs reminders that flimsy toys will break. Karen can monitor his impulse spending without criticizing by making positive comments like, "Gosh, that last plastic squirt gun you bought didn't even last a day without breaking. You need a good squirt gun! Maybe you should think about saving up for a better one next time." If Karen takes the time to coach him at age ten, he will make good progress in becoming a better money manager and avoid more costly lessons later.

Like Karen, you probably already know which of your children needs more time and encouragement to learn about money. You may need to show one child over and over again how to set the table, while another child may need to be shown only once. Likewise, in handling money, some kids need gentle reminders over and over again.

In just eight years, Michael and Sarah will graduate from high school and head out into the world. When you are absorbed in parenthood, as Karen is, you think that eight years is an eternity. From my vantage point at the other end, I can tell you that the time slips by at an astounding rate. Time to prepare our children for the world is very short. Use it well.

Whatever your children's natural tendencies, be supportive and nurturing. A Sarah may be easier to train in matters of money, but sometimes the energy and creativity of a Michael make for the most successful investment bankers. You just have to provide the missing elements.

¢ *Use this system for ages 5 to 18 and beyond*
¢ *Take into consideration the different personalities of your children*

Chapter 3

Some Ground Rules

Before you dole out money to your child, be sure you establish your expectations concerning what, if anything, you expect from her. In the adult world for which you are preparing your child, money involves responsibility, both in earning and in spending or saving. How much your child can learn about these things at any particular point is best decided by you. If you are in a dual-parent household, it is best if you and your spouse make a joint decision about your expectations. As a single parent you will make your own decision, but perhaps talking to other parents will provide you with some helpful feedback. Don't be afraid to establish your own "over the fence" advice network. The good thing about free advice is you don't have to buy it.

In setting some ground rules, start with the earning of the allowance by asking yourself the following questions:

- Should chores be done in exchange for allowance money?

- Should chores be done as a part of family participation with no connection to allowance?

- Should my child be paid for some chores but not others?

- Should an allowance be given with no conditions attached?

Before settling on your answers, remember that determining the boundaries of the allowance experience is more important than whether or not your child should be paid for chores. Perhaps you would rather focus on teaching the management of the money, not the earning. It's your classroom. You decide.

What if you have a spouse who disagrees with you over the answers? Discuss your differences in private so that you can present a consistent focus for your child. Your agreement is very important for your child's learning without confusion. Remind yourselves that you can't teach everything about money at once. Be willing to start small.

Parents have long debated about whether an allowance should be connected to chores. Again, I think the answer depends on the lesson you want to teach. I see no problem in a compromise. Some chores can be done because children have a responsibility to be contributing members of the family. Other chores can be done for pay. Each option teaches a different lesson.

For example, you might expect your child to make the bed and keep her room neat with no pay involved. At the same time you could pay her for setting the table, taking out the trash, washing the car, doing laundry, or mowing the lawns. This way your child can learn both family responsibility and the value of work for pay.

Once she has the money, you will want to consider her need to learn money management. Here are some questions concerning money handling that you can consider in establishing the ground rules:

- Should the money be connected to expected behavior?

- Should part of the allowance be saved?

- Should part of the money be shared?

- How much should be available for spending?

- How much should the decision be left to the child?

Again, I believe that the best answer combines the different possibilities: spending, saving, and sharing. But remember, you set the rules. There is no single right or wrong answer. Only you can balance your values with your child's abilities and needs, coming up with a plan that works for your family.

I would caution you, however, about tying money to behavior. As tempted as we are sometimes to bribe our children with money for good behavior, I believe money is best left out of the issue. Otherwise you may end up teaching a lesson you did not intend, such as how to use behavior to manipulate others for financial gain. You don't want to produce a fourteen-year-old who asks, "How much will you pay me if I sit still through Katie's piano recital?" Instead, let your child know that you expect good behavior; it's not something you pay for.

I will discuss my suggestions for saving part of the allowance later in the book when I break the allowance issues down by age level. I have also included a chapter on a "Post-High School Fund" that includes savings. Also in the age-specific chapters, you'll find unique stories on spending and sharing. Use whatever information fits your family plan.

¢ *Establish your expectations about the money*

¢ *Ask yourself questions about the earning of the allowance*

¢ *Decide what principles you want to teach about money management*

¢ *Beware of the pitfalls of tying money to behavior*

Chapter 4

Our Family Philosophy

I'm going to share with you how my husband Dave and I sorted out the ground rules and decided to handle money with our three children. Your priorities may be different from ours, so your system may differ as well. Take our experience as one possible successful example.

Dave wanted the children to receive a regular allowance beginning at age five. He felt it was important for them to begin learning about sharing, spending, and saving. At this young age, he did not see a need to connect the money to any kind of chore or work to earn it because the lessons he wanted to teach did not require that.

I also wanted the children to learn the same three lessons, but I was hesitant about just handing them money. I didn't want them to think that money is easily acquired or that there is an endless supply. I suspected that such a message would be an unintended lesson of an allowance that isn't earned.

In discussing our different perspectives, Dave and I realized we both agreed there should be a spirit of cooperation within the household with everyone pitching in to help. Dave didn't want this spirit connected to money, and I agreed. On the other hand, I didn't want money disconnected altogether from the idea of work, even if that was not the primary lesson at the early ages. Dave understood my reasoning.

Based on our discussions, we compromised and decided on a plan that blended both of our philosophies.

Together we came up with an approach more balanced than either of us would have developed alone. (Those of you who are single parents may be more resourceful than we were by ourselves. You so often have to be! Still, it may be helpful to bounce your plan off other parents you know in order to check your perspective. Networking is not just for businesses.)

The first stage of our plan began when the kids were toddlers. We introduced cooperation in doing household tasks. Every night we had "toy brigade" where everyone shuttled toys back into the toy box and helped pick up the house. We got participation because we made it fun for the children by marching and singing while cleaning up. Dave was often down on all fours toting our youngest child on his back to carry a stuffed animal back to the toy box. It was silly stuff, but it was good family time and got the clean-up job done in a matter of minutes with everyone participating.

From this toddler period on, and as maturity permitted, the children helped with all sorts of household tasks when we asked them to. They raked leaves (and jumped into the piles), folded laundry, helped with backyard barbecues, swept floors, cleaned the tropical fish bowls, and generally kept the pet rat, snake, guinea pigs and tarantula (don't ask . . .) under control. We were satisfied because we felt they were growing up with a strong sense of family interaction and mutual responsibility. It was natural for them to help out with no expectation of payment.

Allowance Begins

When the children turned five, we began giving them a small amount of money each week with no strings attached, meaning no set financial responsibilities. We encouraged them to put some of it in the church collection plate and to put some in their piggy banks. The remainder was for spending. At the same time, we continued to ask them for help with small household tasks, and we continued to expect their cooperation in doing them.

Expectations were an important key in our household. The children grew up knowing that we had certain expectations for them, not only to help with routine household jobs, but also to have good behavior and to do well in school.

Work for Pay

Around age six, we began a business-like arrangement with the children by paying them a weekly allowance. Part of the allowance was the children's share of the family income, and part was for doing certain jobs. (I have listed suggested allowance amounts and jobs under each age group, beginning in Chapter 7.) A small percentage of the money was designated for saving and sharing, and the children could spend the balance.

The jobs for which we paid the children were separate from the normal expectations that they keep their rooms neat and pick up their toys. The paid jobs were geared toward their abilities and were very simple as befit their age. To add some variety and make things fair for everyone, we rotated the paid jobs so that one child was not always doing the same job.

If the children didn't complete their work-for-pay jobs, we'd remind them once, and, if necessary, twice. If we had to remind them a third time, we docked a part of their allowances. We called it our "once, twice, and three times you're out" system. We told them that they were out part of the allowance because we were out of patience. No harsh words were exchanged, and we assured them that we still loved them, but that not doing a paid job simply leads to not being paid. It was a logical consequence that they needed to learn.

We didn't have to dock them too many times before they stopped ignoring their work. After all, they wanted to receive the full allowance.

Because we were patient and divided the different lessons over time — family responsibility first, then money handling, then work for pay — we were able to address both my concerns and Dave's. Our expectations would only have conflicted if we had tried to do everything at once.

Whether or not you have a parenting partner with whom you must compromise, be willing to teach your children about money in increments. Let one lesson build on the last. These three stages were the beginning of a gradual progression that eventually led to financial independence for our children as well as a healthy reserve of self-esteem.

Some people may look at your success with your young children and think, "That's all well and good, but wait until they become teenagers!" Dave and I found that the spirit of family cooperation that we instilled at an early age carried over into the teen years. As teenagers, our kids rarely reneged on helping out when we asked, although it sometimes took more negotiation at that age. During high school, for example, our son never refused to clean out the car and wash it when we asked. Instead, he would often negotiate to do it later. I remember some nights when he washed the car in the driveway when it was nearly dark. It wasn't a high-quality job, but he did get it done as promised.

Overall, Dave and I have been very pleased with the way our children have handled their money and the work associated with it. Looking back, we are happy we were willing to compromise and take the lessons step by step. I am confident that, with planning, you will one day be able to look back with the same sense of pride at the success of your own financial teaching.

¢ *Establish a philosophy about money*
¢ *Start allowances at age five*
¢ *Introduce the work-for-pay concept*
¢ *Encourage the spirit of family cooperation*

Chapter 5

Expectations

At 7:24 am Andy discovered that he didn't have any lunch money left. He hurriedly started throwing a sandwich together. At 7:25 the school bus chugged up the hill and tooted at the end of Andy's driveway. When the bus driver tooted a second time, eleven-year-old Andy gave up on the sandwich, sprinted into his room, grabbed some of his allowance money, and ran for the bus. His mom didn't say a word. She just looked up at the ceiling and said, "Lord, give me patience!" She thought about the money she had given him at the beginning of the month, enough to buy school lunches for half of the days and milk money only for the other half. She wanted him to pack his lunch on half of the days. She had given him the lump sum for the entire month because she was tired of being hounded for lunch money as the school bus was pulling up each morning.

Unfortunately, Andy spent most of the money on junk food at the local convenience store. He now had to dip into his allowance money to buy school lunches, or he had to bring his lunch from home every day.

Andy's mom sat him down that evening to talk about the money. "Andy, I'm not angry about the money. I am disappointed, though, that you spent so much on junk food. It costs so much and is not very good for you. Now you have to use your allowance money on lunches."

It was clear that Andy was not happy about his money situation either. His mom offered to help him budget better by allotting his lunch money half a month at a time. If he still ran out, it was agreed she would give him a week's lunch money at a time. They discussed the fact that food that is better for him is also cheaper than what he had been buying. She showed him how her expectations could be a solution to his problem.

At the same time, Andy's mom understood her son's hankering for junk food, so she occasionally supplied a candy bar along with fresh fruit for the days he packed a lunch from home. She made a point of keeping his favorite sandwich ingredients on hand. When she saw him packing nutritious food, she took the opportunity to compliment him. She also slipped him a few articles on nutrition and performance from sports magazines. All of these little nudges helped reinforce her expectations.

When Andy saw how serious his mother was about expecting him to eat well, his habits began to turn around. He still liked junk food, but he cut back on it and learned to budget his money at the same time.

Expectations are the likely outcomes we look forward to and believe will happen. Our expectations for our children can be positive or negative. Parents who expect their children to fail often see those expectations come true. But if you expect your child to succeed, you will most often not be disappointed. He will intuitively know your expectations and be encouraged and motivated by them.

Just like Andy's mom, you will have lots of opportunities to nurture your children and let them know your expectations for them. If you gently encourage them by saying, "I know you can do better," they will often meet your expectations. It won't happen overnight because children take months to change their ways. You will need lots of patience. But keep your expectations high and try not to show your total amazement when they finally come around.

When Andy began passing up the snack cakes and reached for the bananas and apples, his mother wanted to jump in the air and click her heels. But she just smiled and for a quiet moment savored her steadfast parenting skills.

Take a Lesson from a Teacher

Teachers are constantly setting high expectations for their students. You can set the same high expectations for how your children manage money.

The true-life experiences of Los Angeles high school teacher Jaime Escalante, in the movie *Stand and Deliver*, exemplify the value of expectations. As an educator, he refused to write off as losers the eighteen inner-city students in his math class. He expected them to succeed and find their ticket out of the barrio. By constantly maintaining high expectations, he motivated them to pass the National Advanced Placement Calculus Exam. His success with the students is inspiring. If you have not seen this movie, I suggest you rent it.

You can model your expectations regarding children and money on this example to achieve the same success. If you maintain high expectations for your children to learn money management, they will rise to the occasion. Children are far more capable of rising to our expectations that we give them credit for.

Should We Pay for School Grades?

It was a beautiful Saturday afternoon as we drove our daughter and several of her school friends to a birthday party. One of them suddenly said, "Guess what! My dad's paying me $10 for every A that I get on my report card!"

My husband shot a glance at me and I took a deep breath. We knew our daughter would pose the money question to us next.

I thought to myself, "This parenting stuff is not easy. We're going to have to set another precedent for our household."

Most of us have slipped our children a few dollars here and there for rewards on school work and other projects. But constant rewards can get expensive and also detract from the child's sense of accomplishment for doing well in school, which should be the real reward. Money might motivate some children, but it can also become their only objective.

You'll have to decide what is comfortable for you. I have friends who do reward their children with money for school grades. As one mom said, "My daughter really responds to money."

It might be wiser to take a simpler and less expensive route if you feel you want to give rewards. After watching your ten-year-old struggle while writing a report, for example, you can acknowledge his efforts by saying, "You've worked really hard on that report. I'm taking you out for a hot fudge sundae."

In our family, we felt it was better to expect our children to gain knowledge for the sheer pleasure of it rather than to make money. Our discussion about the matter prompted us to think of a way to say "Good job!" to acknowledge their school efforts.

So we decided that, about twice a year during their elementary school days, we would let them choose either a family outing or a purchase at the local bookstore as a way of saying to them, "Well done!" This didn't mean they'd earned all As and Bs. It meant we felt they had done their best, no matter what the grade.

The family outing was usually a night out for pizza, an afternoon of miniature golf, a movie, or bowling. The purchase at the bookstore, however, became their favorite pat on the back. We let them choose any book they wanted from anywhere in the bookstore (within reason). They chose everything from games and puzzle books to mysteries and books on tropical fish, cartooning, coin collecting, antique bottles, card tricks, and sports legends. One of them chose a *1909 Sears Roebuck Consumers Guide* catalog. He was fascinated with the items that sold so long ago.

Letting them loose in the bookstore educated us as well. We had no idea they were interested in some of these subjects. It was good family time for all of us.

Having high expectations for your children is so important. Whether they are learning to manage money, achieve in school, kick a soccer ball, or drive the family car, the expectations you have for them can spur them on.

¢ *Maintain high expectations for your children*

¢ *See the movie* Stand and Deliver — *it exemplifies the value of expectations*

¢ *Decide if you want to give rewards for school grades*

Chapter 6

Ages 2 to 4: Groundwork

It's time to start looking at the allowance plan step by step, age by age. Here's where it gets fun.

Dave and I began the groundwork when our children reached age two. Not a whole lot of understanding about money occurs at this age, but there is the all-important concept of family participation, which young toddlers view with excitement. Children find themselves wanting to participate in the world around them, and most of their world consists of the family.

It was a busy Saturday morning, and Gretchen was hurriedly vacuuming her living room carpet with her mind already moving ahead to the other tasks that lay before her. Three-year-old Lindsay toddled into the room and reached for the vacuum arm in order to help Mommy clean. Pulling the vacuum to one side, Gretchen shouted over the drone of the machine, "No, honey, Mommy's in a hurry. You can't help." But Lindsay was not to be put off. She wanted to help. Anticipating a struggle, Gretchen thought, "Okay, it will be easier if I let her have a turn. She probably won't be able to push the vacuum, anyway, and she'll lose interest."

Gretchen stepped back and watched as Lindsay began to push the vacuum a few feet. Suddenly, there was a harsh clanking sound followed by a high-pitched screech from the motor, then silence. Lindsay had attempted to vacuum up a pile of pennies she had been playing with on the carpet the night before.

Aside from the cost of vacuum cleaner repairs, there are two important and very positive things to recognize here. First, the pennies were left on the carpet because of Lindsay's curiosity about money. The night before, she had enjoyed playing with them and stacking them. She's in the beginning stages of learning about money, although not a lot of understanding happens at this young age. If shown a penny, a nickel, and a dime, she'll probably choose the nickel because it's biggest. Abstract concepts about money just don't occur yet.

The second important thing to understand is that preschoolers love to help you, and they have no concept of connecting their help to getting paid. They are eager to do the chores that you are doing. Take advantage of their willingness when you can, and let them participate. You'll be teaching them that their contributions to the family are important. At the same time, you'll be laying the groundwork for teaching them that chores can be fun and are part of your family culture.

You will have to adjust your expectations to what little hands and short attention spans can accomplish. You will also need to give them guidance. All jobs with little ones around take much longer to complete. Instead of becoming frustrated, realize that the time you invest now with preschoolers is laying the foundation for teaching them about family participation and bigger chores as they get older.

You can help lay this foundation if you accept the fact that there are going to be interruptions if young children are around. Take advantage of those interruptions. If you are dusting, give them a rag so they can "dust." If you're making cookies, give them a little dough so they can do their "baking." In less than a minute, they'll probably be off to something else. If it's paperwork you need done, give them crayons and paper. You may get a little more done than if you didn't let them "help" at all, and they'll have fun "helping" you.

Because of safety concerns, of couse, some jobs can't involve little ones. But when you're not too rushed and there's no danger, let them help.

Why should you do this? Because you will ingrain at a young age a habit of family participation that has no connection to money. You'll thank yourself when they are teenagers. I know I did.

¢ *Acknowledge your child's curiosity about money and let her play with a few coins*

¢ *Let preschoolers help with chores to establish the habit of family participation at a young age*

Chapter 7

Age 5:
Money + Guidance

At around age five, children start to express an interest in money. They have made the connection that money buys things. You can begin to take opportunities to give them guidance about how it is handled, such as letting them hand the money to the store clerk when you are shopping. Be prepared for some "missing the concept" at the beginning.

Nancy pulled into the Quik-Mart store and handed Jason, her ten-year-old, a twenty-dollar bill so he could run in and get a half gallon of milk. "I wanna give them the money!" shouted five-year-old Jerry from the back seat. Seeing an opportunity in Jerry's enthusiasm, Nancy replied, "Okay, you can go with your brother, but don't lose the money."

Well, there's losing and then there's losing. Though she wisely cautioned Jerry, Nancy, like all of us, couldn't anticipate every possibility. As the boys returned to the car, older brother Jason staggered with fits of laughter. "You'll never guess what he did. He gave the guy the twenty-dollar bill and didn't even wait for the change!"

Jerry looked confused. After all, he had not lost the money. Amused, Nancy took the time to give Jerry a little lesson on the way money works.

Because five-year-olds are fascinated by money, you can begin teaching them some of the basics of money transactions. You can also watch them experience the pleasure of having some of their own. Try to keep money handling a positive experience. As your child begins to show signs of being able to keep track of money, you can start giving him an allowance. The weekly amount will probably be between one dollar and five dollars, depending on the maturity of your child and the extent of your budget.

Small lessons about responsibility and decision making start here. They learn that once money is spent, it isn't coming back. They learn that they can save it or give it away, as well as spend it. On shopping trips, they can learn how to make a purchase, including counting their money, waiting for change,1 and counting the change. They begin to understand the concept of ownership.

Because kids at this age begin to see the relationship between money and other things, it is a good age to let them see you depositing money in the bank. They can learn that the bank will hold money for you. This can reinforce the early concept of saving. They also learn that you must deposit money into the bank before you can take it out of the wall with your ATM card. It's not too soon to start demystifying the plastic card.

At this age, some children still enjoy collecting money just to have a pile of coins. They amuse themselves counting and sorting them. You can use this tendency by beginning to talk about saving and sharing. The early understanding of saving may simply involve their keeping some of the coins in hand, or putting some in a piggy bank or coin book. Sharing can involve something as simple as buying a pack of gum for a sibling or tossing a couple of coins into the church collection plate (which can be particularly motivating because it is public, communal, active, and "adult").

The seeds of sharing and saving that are planted at this early age will, if tended, grow and lead to good habits later.

If you feel, as Dave did, that age five is too young to hinge any specific job to receiving the allowance, you can connect the allowance payment to being "a good helper" in a general sense. This will set the foundation for the idea of work for pay without emphasizing the point or distracting from the main lessons of simply handling money.

Here's a chart to help you get started and some suggested "Good Helper" tasks suitable to this age.

Age	Weekly Allowance	"Good Helper" Tasks
Around 5	$1 to $5	Help pick up toys
		Answer the phone
		Set the table (with help)
		Clear own place at the table
		Make bed (neatness will come later)
		Get dressed for school
		Pull sheets off bed for laundry
		Help carry in favorite grocery items, such as cereal and cookies, from the car

¢ *Begin to teach how money works*
¢ *Start a regular allowance*
¢ *Talk about simple saving and sharing concepts*
¢ *Hinge the allowance money on "Good Helper" tasks, if you wish*

Chapter 8

Ages 6 to 8: Money + Guidance + Responsibility

As your children move out of the early childhood years, you will notice a greater interest in money and what it will buy. As they become more conscious of peers and popular styles, whether clothes or toys or video games, their motivation to acquire things increases too. Although there are many pitfalls for kids at this age in our consumer society (see Chapter 10), you can take advantage of this increased desire to use money by tying it to increased responsibility. With their greater maturity and greater motivation, they'll now be able to handle some financial responsibility without losing heart or interest.

By age six, most children want to receive an allowance. They want the decision-making power that comes with having their own money. They are also beginning to understand that they can save up for a future purchase. If you feel your child is ready and you wish to teach the lesson, now is the time to tie the allowance to the concept of earning money through work. It is also an opportune time to start giving him power over the use of the money once it is earned.

Six-year-old Gary had started earning a weekly allowance. As his grandfather's birthday approached, his mom reminded him, "Grandpa's birthday is coming." Gary loved his grandpa and intended to buy him a gift, but he impulsively spent all of his allowance money on comic books. Faced with the dilemma he had created, he came up with a quick solution.

Grandpa looked a little puzzled and amused after his birthday dinner when he unwrapped Gary's gift. Under the wrapping paper was a slightly tattered comic book.

When you first add financial responsibilities to your child's allowance, you are giving him his first taste of money management. Be sure to start small so that you don't overwhelm him. Be aware, too, that he may fumble a bit in his first attempts to take charge. Gary's lack of money management in not saving for his grandfather's birthday gift was one small lesson for him in learning to plan ahead. He may still forget to plan for other gifts in the future, but sooner or later he'll learn to set aside a little money. Gary's mom can coax him along by reminding him that birthday gifts don't always have to cost money.

Gary can give Grandpa a "coupon" good for **One Free Car Wash** or **One Hour of Weeding.** Freedom to learn means freedom to fail as well as succeed. Give him the space to learn in these early training years. If you try to force his success, it won't be *his* success.

Earning Allowance Money

Most parents agree that some of the allowance money should be earned in one way or another at this age level. If there are specific jobs to be done in order to receive the money, be clear on what those jobs are. What some parents call family participation, other parents will call jobs. One family might pay for beds to be made and rooms to be kept neat. Another family will consider these chores to be family participation with no payment involved. There are no right or wrong jobs. The lesson is in the earning, not in the nature of the task, so do what makes you feel comfortable.

You will probably have a good idea which task your child can handle, but be aware that he needs your encouragement and supervision to get him started and to sustain him to completion. Plan to work with him at first, and give him lots of praise, even if the job isn't done to your standards. He may have trouble making his bed well, for example, but don't worry if it doesn't look neat. You can help him smooth out the wrinkles later when he has more experience.

You will need lots of patience when you start giving him jobs that are connected to money. At this age, he needs reminders over and over again to do his work. Getting angry when he forgets doesn't help. Taking him by the hand and explaining that you need him to do this job if he wants the money will produce results. The consequences of his working or not working will not be your feelings, but rather the concrete reward of money. Be flexible as you guide him along and try to make this work-for-pay introduction a positive time.

Learning to Spend

Children have to learn to spend before they can understand the concept of saving. We save in order to spend more wisely or more profitably or just later. Children who learn to spend well begin to see money as a tool for achieving what they want. They learn to make the choices about how that money is used. Saving money can then be a logical extension of the spending process. It is simply another way to use the tool of money.

Learning to Save

Putting money in a bank where it can't be seen or touched may be too abstract an undertaking for a child of this age. They tend to forget the things that are not nearby. However, a child of six or seven will enjoy saving money in a glass jar or a piggy bank where it is visible and close at hand.

At this age, the rewards for saving money should be direct and concrete. You can show your child how to save for a particular toy or a special outing. Keep in mind that a six-year-old can only understand planning ahead for a short time, so don't expect him to accumulate savings for college or some other long-term goal.

As a way of encouraging saving, you may want to consider offering to match the amount saved, the way philanthropists often match charity funds raised. This can eventually lead to an understanding of the way banks reward saving by paying interest.

To help your little saver keep interest (pun intended, of course), find ways to make the process real and concrete. Let's say your son wants a toy truck that costs three dollars, and he decides to save fifty cents a week matched by your fifty cents, for a weekly total of one dollar. Make a simple chart showing how many weeks it will take to save up for the truck and stick it on your refrigerator. Putting it in a visible place will remind him of his goal.

Then give him an old wallet or a container with a lid in which to collect the money. Every week, when he saves the money, let him check it off on the chart. With your help, he can enjoy figuring out the time left and recording the money saved.

Now suppose your child wants to buy lots of things rather than having his heart set on one toy. Again, keeping the whole process visible and concrete, write down the items desired on separate slips of paper and put those slips in a jar. When he has saved enough to make a purchase, he can choose one of the items in the jar.

Delayed Gratification

Learning to save money, whether it's for a toy or a night at the local pizza parlor, teaches a child delayed gratification. This means he learns to accept the time interval between the wish for the toy truck and the actual purchase of the toy. In fact, he begins to see the time as a natural part of the process.

With the cost of living what it is today, children often find that they don't immediately have enough funds to buy what they want. They are forced to save, and that is good. Children who learn that they can't have all of their wishes granted on the spot are learning that there are roadblocks in life. More importantly, they are learning that, with a little patience, work, and time, such roadblocks can be overcome. Lack of immediate gratification becomes a challenge to be met rather than a source of frustration. How many of us wish we had learned delayed gratification before we reached adulthood!

Ages six to eight are years for a little allowance and a lot of gentle guidance. Financial responsibilities such as purchasing decisions should be kept simple. And because children at this age are just beginning to grasp the concepts of saving and spending, don't expect too much consistency. That will come in time.

Age	Weekly Allowance	Suggested Jobs*
6 to 8	$2 to $5**	Set the table
		Pick up belongings
		Hang up clothes
		Care for a pet
		Make bed
		Clear the table
		Empty wastebaskets
		Keep room neat

* Specify which jobs you are paying for and which ones are part of family participation (no payment).

** This is the range for basic allowance. You can pay them extra money for completion of jobs and for milk or lunch money, bus fare, and so on. For example, a 7-year-old might get:

Weekly allowance	$2.00
Payment for jobs	$2.00
(maybe setting table, caring for a pet)	
Bus fare	$2.50
Weekly total	**$6.50**

¢ *Connect some small financial responsibilities to the allowance money*

¢ *Let them earn some of the allowance money*

¢ *Teach them about spending choices*

¢ *Show them how to save up for something they want*

¢ *Teach them delayed gratification*

Chapter 9

Ages 9 to 11: Money + Guidance + More Responsibility

Once children reach the age of nine or thereabouts, they begin to have the capacity to understand how the more abstract concepts of saving, spending, giving, and budgeting relate to their concrete, real-life needs, desires, and actions. If they have had some early training already, the transition into greater financial responsibility will not be too difficult. Still, you will need to stay close to provide guidance. When children are learning new ideas and behaviors, it's always a little awkward at first.

It was Saturday morning, and Eric was at the breakfast table getting his weekly allowance from Mom. She smiled at him and pushed a wild tuft of hair off his forehead. She had decided that Eric was old enough to take on more financial responsibility, and as a single parent with a full-time job, she recognized that his doing so would be a benefit to them as a family. "I'm giving you ten dollars extra today in your allowance so you can go get a haircut this week," she explained.

The following Saturday, when it was once again allowance time, Eric's hair was looking even shaggier. His mom noticed, despite his careful attempts to comb it back.

"Why didn't you get your hair cut this week?" she asked.

"I didn't have enough money," he replied.

"But I gave you ten dollars last Saturday. What did you do with the money?" she quizzed.

Looking rather sheepish, he explained that he had spent the extra money on video games.

Scenes like this will happen when you begin letting your children have more financial responsibility. In Eric's case, his mom let him know firmly that the money was not to be squandered. That afternoon, with his current allowance and a few dollars from savings, he scraped together enough to go get his hair cut.

You can't expect your child to be a responsible money manager overnight because budgeting techniques have to be learned. As your child's maturity permits, however, you can add small budgeting responsibilities to the weekly allowance. For example, if your child needs money for school supplies, lunches, transportation, haircuts, gifts, or the like, you can dole out that extra money at allowance time. It is his responsibility to ration the money for these items. This responsibility is important because it prepares him for the next big step in budgeting at the junior high level.

Remember, these are your child's formative money management years. It's important for him to learn about handling money before he reaches the challenging junior high age. This is the time to give him lots of suggestions and guidance regarding spending, sharing, and saving.

Ages nine to eleven are also when a child starts lobbying for more allowance. He may broach the subject by saying his friend, Bobby, gets $25 per week for allowance. It probably isn't so (Bobby is likely to be boasting). This is an opportunity for you to suggest that if he really wants more allowance, he can take on another household job to earn extra money.

Opening a Savings Account

If your child doesn't have a savings account yet, this is a good age to help her open one. Check with your bank to see if there is a minimum deposit necessary to start an account. Talk to your child about saving up that amount for this important financial step.

Explain to her that the bank will pay her interest for the use of her money. Furthermore, the bank continues to pay interest on the interest earned, and this is called compounding. Impress upon her that it's such a good deal that financiers have described compounding as the "eighth wonder of the world."

Show her the following chart from Harold and Sandy Moe's book, *Teach Your Child the Value of Money*. It shows how her money can build if she puts just one dollar in a compounding account. Of course, there's no bank that would let her start an account with just one dollar, but this illustrates what a good deal compounding is.

One Dollar Earning Compound Interest

End of Year:	Interest Rate								
	3%	5%	6%	8%	10%	12%	14%	16%	18%
1	1.03	1.05	1.06	1.08	1.10	1.12	1.14	1.16	1.18
5	1.16	1.28	1.34	1.47	1.61	1.76	1.93	2.10	2.29
10	1.34	1.63	1.79	2.16	2.59	3.11	3.71	4.41	5.23
15	1.56	2.08	2.40	3.17	4.18	5.47	7.14	9.27	11.97
20	1.81	2.65	3.21	4.66	6.73	9.65	13.74	19.46	27.39
25	2.09	3.39	4.29	6.85	10.83	17.00	26.46	40.87	62.67
30	2.43	4.32	5.74	10.06	17.45	29.96	50.95	85.85	143.37
35	2.81	5.52	7.69	14.79	28.10	52.80	98.10	180.31	328.00
40	3.26	7.04	10.29	21.72	45.26	93.05	188.88	378.72	750.38
45	3.78	8.99	13.76	31.92	72.89	163.99	363.68	795.44	1716.68
50	4.38	11.47	18.42	46.90	117.39	289.00	700.23	1670.70	3927.36

Now ask her if she can imagine how much money she could accumulate if she saved one dollar per week in a compounding savings account. Explain that in a savings account, her money will be working to earn her more money, and that she doesn't have to do a thing except leave it in.

Let her know that, although there are advantages to leaving the money in savings, she still has control over her money. She can take it out any time she wants, with the exception of funds earmarked for a specific purpose.

One Family's Plan

Here's how one couple I know began the savings process. They showed their daughter how to divide up her $5.00 per week allowance to ensure that part of it went into savings:

10% tithing and giving	=	$ 0.50
20% savings	=	$ 1.00
70% to keep (spend)	=	$ 3.50
Total	=	**$ 5.00**

They provided her with envelopes for each category of money to help her keep her money separated. They were not surprised when their daughter forgot now and then about tithing and saving. They simply provided a gentle reminder. They recognized that a child her age still needs a great deal of guidance. A few simple forms of parental guidance helped the daughter begin a real-life experience of saving money. Though they gave her room for trial-and-error growth, they continued to remind her of their expectations that she save part of her money.

Sharing with Others

There may be a tendency, with an allowance system for a child, to lean toward concentrating solely on his needs and wants. Here's how one family encouraged their children to share a portion of their savings to help others:

> The three brothers were sprawled on the living room floor with all the money from the shoe box dumped in a pile. Ben, the oldest, was counting it again . . . "forty-six, forty-seven, forty-eight!"
>
> "Okay, so by next week, we'll have enough," said the youngest, as they proudly admired their stack of bills.

These boys' parents had set up an allowance system that put an emphasis on giving. They paid their sons five dollars per week allowance: one dollar for church, two dollars to save, and two dollars to spend. Each week the boys put the two dollars that were be saved into the shoe box. When they had accumulated fifty dollars total, they could decide where to donate this money. They figured that with this larger amount, it really could make a difference.

They had a lot of fun each week clustered around the shoe box, counting the money and discussing how it should be used. Sometimes they sent it to UNICEF, and sometimes it went to the local food kitchen. Once they sent it to a youth organization that was raising money to install a basketball hoop in the park.

Teaching your children to share some of their money with those who are less fortunate lays the groundwork for producing adults who are generous and caring toward others. The best teacher for this is you because children learn by example. You don't have to donate large sums of money. Just letting your children see you put a dollar in the Salvation Army bucket speaks louder than words.

The Post-High School Fund

Because of the increased ability to handle abstract ideas at this age, nine to eleven is a good time to help your child begin a long-term savings program. With such a program you can reinforce your expectations by guiding her in setting long-term goals and in planning for her education beyond high school.

To accomplish these things with our three children, we had each of them contribute a portion of the allowance to a savings account that we called the Post-High School Fund. Setting aside this money taught them self-discipline and helped them focus on some future goals, specifically college or trade school.

We earmarked the money in the fund for covering each child's personal expenses during the first year of college or trade school. If any one of them decided not to continue an education beyond high school, we agreed that the money should be used to launch that child into the work force. It could cover transportation, training costs, tools, and uniforms. It could also provide start-up costs for her own business.

Here's how we set up the fund. Let's say our nine-year-old was getting three dollars per week as a basic allowance and an additional dollar for doing odd jobs. (I've updated these amounts to more current levels; I won't date myself by telling you what the original amounts for our children were.) We then added two dollars a week to establish the Post-High School Fund. Her allowance looked like this:

Basic allowance:	$3.00
Extra jobs:	$1.00
Post-High School Fund:	$2.00
Total:	**$6.00**

Obviously, two dollars a week wasn't going to put a big dent in her college costs. For this reason, we established a separate, larger college fund to which we contributed on a regular basis. The Post-High School Fund was primarily for the financial training of the children. Through it they learned the habit of regular savings, and they learned to save with a purpose. Also, the fund was set up to cover only personal expenses during the first year of college, not all college costs. We wanted to remove the pressure to find a job in the freshman year. The focus of the fund and the amount of the deposit can be adjusted to fit your own expectations.

In order to teach another practical skill through the fund — budgeting — we set up the deposit system in a way that put as much of the responsibility on the child as possible. The first week, we gave her an extra two dollars and told her that we would need to collect that two dollars back each week, starting the following week. It was her job to be a good steward of the money so that it would still be available when we collected it in a week for deposit in her Post-High School Fund.

Why didn't we just take an automatic deduction of two dollars from her allowance each week and bank it for her? That would not teach her anything about savings or good stewardship of money because we would be doing the saving. Being in charge of the money during the week made her an active participant and taught her self-discipline with money.

I know you're wondering what we did when she spent her allowance during the week and did not have the two dollars to deposit. I could tell you our daughter was perfect and never did such a thing. I could, but I won't. When she neglected to budget and instead spent the entire amount, we gently but firmly reminded her of the importance of regular savings. We then took the two dollars from her current week's allowance and deposited it for her. That left her with a four dollar allowance instead of six, two of which had to be saved for the following week's deposit:

Basic allowance:	$1.00
	($3 less the
	$2 not saved)
Extra jobs:	$1.00
Post-High School Fund:	$2.00
Total:	**$4.00**

Did she forget in future weeks to have the two dollars ready? Yes, sometimes she did. We just kept emphasizing the importance of saving and the need to budget to make that saving possible. Eventually her lapses were very infrequent.

A quick, practical point: to make our lives simpler as far as bookkeeping and to avoid any bank deposit charges, we kept envelopes for our children as they started this savings program. We accumulated a couple months' worth of savings before taking the money to the bank to make the deposits.

A common problem for children starting college is the adjustment to their new schedule and surroundings. If they have to start freshman year with the added responsibility of a part-time job, it might be too much for them to handle. Encouraging them to get their feet wet in the "Study Department" first is good advice.

Most college students are going to have to get parttime jobs at some point to help with the costs. If they can delay this until second semester freshman year or into their sophomore year, their adjustment to college may be easier. Teenagers who work during high school have the advantage of experience in budgeting work/study time, so the transition will be easier for them.

For now, let's see what can happen with this small amount of two dollars per week. Suppose you have a nine-year-old, and you're starting a Post-High School Fund. This child has nine years before high school graduation. At this writing, passbook interest is around 3%. Here is an approximate projection of savings:

$2 per week x 4 weeks per month	= $8 per month
$8 per month x 12 months	= $96 per year
(plus compounded interest)	= $97.44
$96 per year x 9 years	= $864
(plus compounded interest)	= $1,005

So, depending on how the bank compounds the savings, your child could have over a thousand dollars when college begins without ever contributing more than two dollars a week. Realistically, a thousand dollars doesn't go too far, and the two-dollar figure has more to do with choosing a training amount than the actual costs of a college student's personal expenses. To compensate, as children get older, they can contribute more than two dollars a week, and they can branch out into other money vehicles that pay more interest.

As our children matured, we phased out the mandated college savings system. Instead, we asked them to deposit half of their earnings from paper routes, babysitting jobs, and other jobs into their Post-High School Fund. The deposits usually exceeded two dollars a week. To encourage compliance, we often reminded them that they would be responsible for their personal expenses all through college, and their lack of discipline now would deprive them later.

Granted, at age twelve or thirteen, the thought of needing money for college wasn't foremost in their minds (if it was there at all). By age fifteen, however, the light began to dawn, and all three of them began to focus more on their savings. College wasn't something far off; it was coming soon. Because we had started them early, they did not need to start from scratch at this point, but we could turn more and more of the responsibility over to them as their awareness and motivation increased. We had already provided them the tools.

By ages sixteen and seventeen, a couple of them were depositing every dollar from their summer job paychecks into savings. Their earlier lessons about regular savings were paying off. How each of them fared on the Post-High School Fund is covered in Chapter 22, in the "Off to College" section.

Non-College Goals

College doesn't have to be the only reason for a Post-High School Fund. Some children need a goal more specific than one called "college and your future." They identify more with saving up to buy a car, pay for travel, cover a project (like building a go-cart), turn a hobby into a profitable venture, or start an investment program. Regardless of their goals, a small nest egg accumulated through high school graduation not only gives them confidence and self-esteem, but it gives them choices about their future.

A Post-High School Fund with a Twist

One father contributed to a Post-High School Fund for his children from another angle. If, at age sixteen, his children agreed to delay getting their driver's licenses for a couple of years, he would contribute the additional insurance money he saved each year into a Post-High School Fund.

He proposed this because he wasn't thrilled about his children getting driver's licenses as soon as they were eligible to drive. He wanted to see more maturity on their part before they drove off in the family car. After high school graduation, he let them use this money for travel and/or enrichment.

This scenario would work only if you were planning to pay for the auto insurance for your children. Some families have their teenagers pay for part or all of the additional auto insurance.

Branching Out to Other Investments

Even though interest earned on savings accounts today is low, children will still feel good about watching their money grow. Once they accumulate some savings, they can branch out into other types of investments such as mutual funds, stocks, and CDs (certificates of deposit).

For small investors, financial planners suggest buying stock mutual funds (many companies) rather than single-issue stocks (one company) because of the inherent diversification, which makes them less risky. Mutual fund providers may have minimum age requirements for ownership. Therefore, this may dictate your child's introduction to this area of investment. Once established, however, these funds will produce monthly or quarterly statements that will be mailed to your children. Receiving these statements can be the spark that intrigues some children into getting hooked on investing. They begin to take pride in their financial growth.

Most of us are a little (or a lot) uneasy when it comes to investing. We can't risk the chance of losing our money. If you're feeling on thin ice in this area, I'd recommend Janet Bodnar's book, *Kiplinger's Money-Smart Kids (And Parents, Too!)* to get you started. It has a great chapter on investing and shows you how to track stocks and read the stock listings in the paper. She also explains mutual funds, certificates of deposit, money-market mutual funds, and stock mutual funds.

Single-issue stocks are easier for children to understand, especially if it's stock in a company they know. If they own stock in their favorite fast food company, it's more relevant for them. They understand that they actually own a piece of that company (and they may want to eat there all the time). Show them how to find the value of their stock in the newspaper, and let them track the highs and lows.

One of our daughters chose a different type of investment. She purchased certificates of deposit while in high school. CDs pay a higher rate than regular savings accounts, but they require a minimum deposit (usually at least $500), and you can't touch the money for a certain period of time (commonly six months, one year, or longer).

Heidi set up a "laddered" program so she eventually had four two-year CDs with maturity dates staggered six months apart. This allowed her to take interest money every six months without penalty. During her college days, she had to cash in all her CDs, but this savings program served her well.

Whatever investment your children choose, banks today have all kinds of pamphlets loaded with their banking services to help get you started. Financial planners can also help you establish goals, assess risk, and select investment vehicles. Getting your children started in an investment program when they are young is smart planning because they will have time on their side for investment growth.

You can see there's a lot you can begin teaching your children about money at this nine- to eleven-year-old age. When it comes to being generous with money, you are their best example. Also, as you give them more financial responsibility for things like haircuts, school supplies, and gifts for friends, you prepare them for the next step of this allowance system at the junior high level.

Long-term savings like the Post-High School Fund and branching out into other investments can start the wheels turning for planning for their future, even if they're not in first gear yet. If you guide them along, it'll all start to make sense for them as they become teenagers.

Age	Weekly Allowance	Suggested Jobs
9 to 11	$3 to $5*	Help with laundry
		Load dishwasher
		Take out trash
		Vacuum/dust
		Prepare simple meals
		Keep room neat
		Care for a pet
		Bring in trash cans
		Sort recycle items
		Crush cans for recycling

* Additional earnings per week for doing jobs is $5, on average.

A 10-year-old's weekly allowance might be this:

Basic allowance	$3.00
Extra jobs	$3.00
Post-High School Fund (optional)	$2.00
Total	**$8.00**

Plus: Lunch money, school supplies, money for birthday gifts, haircuts (in short, any items you want to give them financial responsibility for)

¢ *Start giving your children more financial responsibility*

¢ *Open a savings account for them*

¢ *Teach generosity now and you will produce a caring adult*

¢ *Start a Post-High School Fund for long-term goals*

¢ *Branch out into other investments*

Chapter 10

Ages 12 to 17: Money + Minimal Guidance + Greater Responsibility

Puberty. Adolescence. The teen years. These are words that strike fear into the hearts of many parents. Believe it or not, this is the age when money matters can become easier for you. For teens, these years are a natural period of breaking away and seeking independence (though their methods are often, shall we say, awkward). A wise parent understands this and doesn't fight it. You want them to learn to be responsible. You want to be able to trust them to handle things well on their own. They want independence. They want respect. Talk about the perfect raw materials for a successful merger! Understand, however, that successful mergers are often preceded by rocky negotiations and clumsy trial periods. As with the other ages in your child's life, you will need to provide patience and guidance.

One challenge at this age is to make your guidance more subtle; otherwise, you work against the goal of independence. You can do this by giving them more of the decision-making power and then acting simply as an advisor. You can also plan strategies so that consequences are tied to the cause-and-effect reality of money matters (such as, if you spent it already, you now have to do without). This takes the focus and the pressure off you. You have already begun to deal with these issues if you have been using this plan since earlier years, but in the teen years the situations can seem more extreme and more aggravating, partly because the amount of money involved increases (what my kids used to call "the big money").

Maybe you've had shopping days with your children that go something like this:

> You take your twelve-year-old son to buy tennis shoes. As you browse the shelves comparing prices, you have a sudden flash memory of those cute little shoes you used to buy at the discount store for your two-year-old, the shoes that were inevitably accepted with an appreciative grin and a hug. Those inexpensive little shoes. Those wonderfully inexpensive little appreciated shoes. You are snapped out of your daydream by the sound of your no-longer-two-year-old son's voice.
>
> "Awesome! These are the ones I want!"
>
> Clutched in his eager hands is a $95 pair of the latest athletic footwear that you had rolled your eyes at moments before. You think you hear the *Jaws* theme begin somewhere in the distance.
>
> "But, son," you try to say calmly, "you'll outgrow those in months. That's a lot of money for two months of shoe." You smile with brave optimism and hand him a $29.95 pair to try on.
>
> "Yuuuuuck!" he groans. "Nobody wears those! I'd be laughed out of school. Everybody else is wearing these."
>
> A pain develops behind your eyes. Your budget cannot handle $95 tennis shoes. Yet you

suddenly have a vision of your son hanging out at some convenience store with a group of other barefoot outcasts who have stashed their $29.95 tennis shoes behind a neighbor's bushes rather than wear them to school.

Peer pressure has taken over, and your twelve-year-old suddenly has champagne tastes.

You can avoid situations like this that turn your trips to the shopping mall into battlegrounds if you have your children on this allowance system. This is the step in the system when you shift into high gear about teaching your children to handle money. It is possible to enjoy hassle-free shopping with them.

The time has come for you to step out of the picture and turn the spending choices over to them. Simply put, you expand their allowance and give them the sum of money that covers all of the items you would normally buy for them. I have provided charts to help you calculate the amount. You can divide this amount to cover one week's expenses, two weeks', or an entire month's. The beauty of it is that they have the responsibility of deciding how to spend the money.

What if they spend the entire month's allowance on video games, or designer jeans, or those $95 tennis shoes?

Some of what we learn as human beings is from instruction, but a great deal of what we learn comes from experience. So, let them experience this system, and let the law of natural consequences run its course. You are gaining freedom from their spending choices, but you must be willing to let them make their own mistakes.

As one mom said, "The hardest part of this system is keeping my mouth shut when my thirteen-year-old buys dumb items. How many black T-shirts do you really need?"

As the months went by, however, her son began to shop smarter. He still made occasional impulsive purchases, but by age fourteen, she saw great improvement in the choices he made. Best of all, the fighting between them had stopped because she had stepped out of the spending decision.

Your children will also learn about quality. If they buy an expensive item that falls apart after a couple of washings, they'll probably want to return it and get their money back. They may also buy expensive, designer clothing at first, but soon they'll learn comparison shopping. You'll see them begin to thrive on making their own spending decisions.

Remember, most children are going to view this responsibility of handling "the big money" as a great privilege, and they will be good stewards of their share of the monthly budget. When it becomes "their" money and they realize it has limits, some amusing things begin to happen.

> Fifteen-year-old Chris bounded into the grocery store. He had been named "High School Athlete of the Week" by our local newspaper and given a $10 gift certificate from a grocery store chain. He was excited about the opportunity to spend $10 on whatever he wanted.
>
> First he grabbed a half gallon of his favorite ice cream and a large box of sugar-coated cereal (the kind his mom refused to buy). He was about to grab a six-pack of soda when he discovered he only had enough money left to buy a pack of gum. He was totally amazed that the $10 was spent. Several times on the way home he exclaimed, "I can't believe this is all I got!"

When children start on this system, the same thing happens. With a limited amount of money, it's almost comical how fast they start to watch prices. It's no longer your money they're spending, but theirs, and it becomes very near and dear to them.

Obviously, this will be a big step for them, as well as for you. You can get off to a good start by setting a few guidelines, which I'll explain on the following pages. All you have to do then is sit back and enjoy watching your children's attitudes about money change as the months unfold. This is a win-win situation because your budgeting for them becomes relatively stress free (a set amount is allotted each month), and they are learning solid money management skills that they will use for a lifetime.

How to Explain This Big Step to Your Child

If you have been gradually adding money and financial responsibilities to your children's allowance from a young age, this won't be a big step for them. If, on the other hand, you are initiating this system without any prior progression, take time to explain this step to them so they can make an easy transition.

Tell them you have a new allowance system that gives them more financial responsibility and privileges. Ask them if they would like to try it.

Whether they are new to this system or not, you need to decide with them what items you expect them to cover with the money you will allot them each pay period. Here are some items for which you may already be doling out money:

Clothes	Cosmetics
Entertainment	Hobbies
School lunches	Haircuts
Fast food/snacks	Yearbooks
Transportation	Gas
Gifts	Movie rental

Donations	Money for dates
School supplies	Computer software/games
Books/comics	Sporting events

Add any items that pertain to your particular situation. You can let them be responsible for all of the items or just a few to begin with. The more responsibility they have, however, the more they will learn.

At age twelve, we gave our children budgeting responsibility for all of these items, with the exception of gas money, which wasn't needed yet. (Thank heavens!) You can continue paying the basic allowance and extra money for jobs if you wish. In our situation, we cut back on allowance and job money at this time because our children were earning money from paper routes, babysitting, and house-cleaning jobs by this age.

It may sound like we gave our children a lump sum of money at twelve and just let them fend for themselves. True, our strategy was to give minimal guidance so that they would learn money management. At the same time, we were always available when they asked for advice, especially in the early teen years when they were new to this system. One of them asked a lot of questions about what she should buy. Another one became very organized and made her own little budget to keep track of her spending. The third one jumped right in, managed the amount given, and never asked for advice. Once again, those different personalities emerged.

Maybe you think this is too much responsibility for your twelve-year-old or young teenager. Or, maybe when you suggest this system, he will say, "That's scary. I don't want to be responsible for all that money."

In this case, you can ease him in by initially giving him responsibility for only a few items, like movies, fast food, gifts, and haircuts. As he grows more comfortable with the system, you can add more responsibilities, like clothing, hobbies, transportation, donations, and entertainment.

Another suggestion for introducing this system comes from a dad whose daughter wanted to be on this plan but was unsure about how well she would manage the money. He kept a small notebook for her at home that listed her balance. He parceled out money as she requested it and kept a running balance of her available funds. After a couple of years, she was more comfortable with her budgeting capabilities and asked for the whole allowance amount at the beginning of the month.

Another suggestion, to get you off to a smooth start, is to avoid beginning this system in the month of September because kids can be overwhelmed with all the back-to-school expenses. You might want to introduce this system during a less "shopping-oriented" time.

In addition, we felt the cost for sports and sports equipment, as well as enrichment classes such as music, art, theater, and dance, deserved special consideration. These items are discussed in Chapter 13.

Figuring Costs

It's very important that you be realistic about your budget estimates at the start. For example, if you and your children estimate that you usually buy about four pairs of jeans for them per year, don't reduce this estimate to two pairs per year. The opposite should also be avoided. Don't estimate ten pairs of jeans just to keep up with the rich kid down the street. (You will hear a lot about this "kid" during the budget formation process.)

If you find it difficult to determine how many items per year, think of the number per month or per season. Ask your children to do a scan of their closets. They'll probably be able to tell you how much clothing you bought for them in the last few months or year. Most children are excited about going on this system and will be eager to give you input. They like the thought of getting "the big money."

Charting Your Plan

I'm including some charts to get you started. You can find many of the prices you need for filling in the chart by glancing at the Sunday newspaper ads. Also, you don't have to fill out the charts in one sitting. You can jot down prices when you come across them. Your checkbook and charge card records and any recent clothing receipts will also be helpful.

If you plan to start this system in a year or so, start saving clothing and shoe receipts now, or just jot down the costs. This will put all the information at your fingertips when you need it.

When filling out the charts, it's important not to be hung up on trying to reach the perfect estimate. Go with your best guess. You can adjust the amount up or down later. The main consideration is that the amount of allowance fits your financial circumstances. Be fair and be realistic.

Depending upon your lifestyle and available income, you might determine that your teenager needs $150 per month to cover the items you have agreed upon. Your neighbor might determine from her family's lifestyle and available income that $75 per month will have to cover the bases. And her teenagers might have to cover some of their expenses with part-time jobs. This is fine — no matter what level of income you have, your children will be learning good money management.

The first chart involves clothing expenses. Because clothing is one of the biggest expenses, I put it on a separate chart. All of the other expenses your children might have are listed on the second chart.

How to Fill in the Charts

Each family will fill in these charts differently. The Unit Price (cost of each item) and the Number per Year (how many are necessary and affordable) will depend on your

CLOTHING

Item	Unit Price	Number Per Year	Total Yearly Cost
Jeans			
Shirts			
Blouses			
T-shirts			
Skirts			
Shorts			
Pants			
Shoes: Sport			
Dress			
Coats/Jackets			
Underwear			
Socks/Nylons			
Pajamas/Robes			
Slippers			
Bathing Suits			
Jewelry			
Accessories: (Includes hats, gloves, sunglasses, belts, neckties, hair adornments)			
Sports: *			
Team Uniforms			
Shoes/Cleats			
Special Events:			
Tuxedo Rentals			
Prom Dresses			
Formal Shoes			
Other:			
Grand Total - Yearly Costs			
Divide by 12			
Total Monthly Allowance			

* You may want to pay for these yourself

OTHER EXPENSES

Item	Unit Price	Number Per Year	Total Yearly Cost
School Supplies *			
School Lunches			
Gifts (Birthday and Holiday)			
Donations			
Haircuts			
Cosmetics			
Hobbies			
Snacks			
Books/Comics			
Transportation			
Money for Dates			
Gas Money			
School Yearbooks			
Movies (include snacks)			
Movie Rentals			
Video Games			
Compact Discs			
Concerts			
Dances			
Sporting Events			
Bowling			
Skating			
Other:			
Grand Total - Yearly Costs			
Divide by 12			
Total Monthly Allowance			

*Items like this are hard to determine,
so just plug in your best estimate

buying habits and your family's financial situation. Some of the items will pertain to your children, and some will not.

Use the charts as a worksheet to figure a monthly allowance. Here's a sample, but put in your own prices and number per year:

Clothing Item	Unit Price	Number per Year	Total Yearly Cost
Jeans	$25	4	$100
T-shirts	$10	6	$ 60

Other Items	Unit Price	Number per Year	Total Yearly Cost
Gifts	$10	8	$ 80
Movies	$5	6*	$ 30

* Less if under 12 years old

Don't be concerned if you are stumped on items like how many gifts per year, or how many movies, or how much for cosmetics. Just plug in an estimate to get you started.

You can tailor the charts to suit your own needs. For example, one mother decided to buy underwear, socks, shoes, and coats for her children. She gave them a monthly allowance to cover the rest of their wardrobe such as jeans, sweaters, T-shirts, and dresses. By doing this, she avoids the arguments over the price of clothes and expensive fads. She feels good about providing them with some of the basics, but leaves the rest of the clothing choices to them. Her shopping days with them are peaceful.

For some households, when teenagers start part-time jobs, parents taper off on the amount of allowance they give. Some teens are expected to buy all of their clothes with money from outside jobs. If this is your situation, you may want to use only the chart labeled "Other Expenses" to determine a monthly allowance.

Perhaps this is a big step and a leap of faith for you
to hand over such a large sum of money to your child.
If so, remember that great risks lead to great rewards.
The lessons he will learn through this will remain
through his lifetime. I think the risk is justified.

Age	Weekly Allowance*	Suggested Jobs * *
12 to 17	$12 to $50 (weekly)	Newspaper route
	or	Yard work/lawn mowing service
	$50 to $200 (monthly)	Painting jobs
		Carpet cleaning
		Shoveling snow
		Washing cars
		Mother's helper at birthday parties
		Babysitting
		Computer lab work (school or business)
		Aiding senior citizens
		Entrepreneurial ventures: - Snowcone business - Recycle collection - Play group for younger kids
		Athletic team assistant
		Store clerk/bookkeeper
		Cashier
		Fast-food employee
		At-home business (hire them yourself)

* You will calculate this amount from the charts. It is
determined by what items you want them to be responsible for.

** They will shift to jobs outside the home in this age group. In addition to the items you selected from the charts, you can continue paying them the basic weekly allowance, or taper it off as they earn outside income.

¢ *Give a large allowance, plus lots of financial responsibility, and minimize your guidance*

¢ *Take time to explain this big step to your child*

¢ *Be realistic about clothing and other items you want them to cover*

¢ *Fill in the charts to determine an allowance amount*

Chapter 11

You Set the Example

You can read all the books you want on teaching children about money. You can gather information from your neighbors and friends about how they are handling the money issue. You can give all sorts of guidance to your children, but the way they see you handling money is their greatest teacher. Your actions and attitudes about money influence them the most.

Do you use money wisely? Do they see you giving contributions to charities? Are you relaxed about money? Do they ever see you planning how to cover the cost of big purchases?

When writing this book, I asked my children what impressions they had about how we, as parents, handled money. One of them recalled a conversation about a car purchase that probably went something like this:

Dave, arriving home late: "I had trouble with the car again today. I don't think we should put any more money into repairs. We're at the point where we need to start thinking about replacing that car."

Judy: "Well, we've just paid off the washer and dryer but we're going to have dental bills for Marc's braces starting next month. And the summer family reunion is coming up. That's going to cost a lot for all of us to go."

Dave: "Yeah, we're going to have to sit down and go over our budget again. We may have to pare down some of our expenses,

because we don't want to dip into savings unless
we really have to."

Conversations like this, although not directed at your
children, can have a great influence on them. They'll grow
up hearing you have discussions about your finances, not
shouting matches. Even though they sense a problem
about how everything is going to be paid for, there's a
relaxed tone in discussing the matter. They pick up on the
fact that planning for major purchases is necessary. They
see you explore other avenues before you consider tap-
ping savings for big items.

In addition, your day-to-day spending habits are
absorbed by your children. They see you buy clothes at
the mall, sporting goods, and tools for your garage. They
love it when you take them to eat out and go to the
movies. They watch you write a check to your favorite
charity. They learn that money is something to be enjoyed
and shared.

On the other hand, if you're always complaining that
you have no money or that you can never get your VISA
card balance paid off, they will absorb this as well. If you
bounce checks because you don't keep track of your checking account balance, they will feel your frustration. They
learn that money is a negative factor that causes stress.

Finding the middle ground for spending should be
your goal. Spend enough to cover necessities and have
some pleasures, but not so much that you get in debt.
They'll be watching and learning, so try to set a good
example as they grow up. By age twelve, their peers are
going to have a great influence on them. This makes it
even more important to lay the groundwork for sensible
money handling at a young age. They are less apt to stray
in adolescence if they've been raised with good guidelines.

¢ *Set a good example about managing money because you are the primary teacher*

¢ *Demonstrate that money is to be shared and enjoyed*

Chapter 12

Keeping Your Allowance System on Track

Now that you have pledged to set a good example about handling money and have filled in the charts to determine a realistic monthly allowance, there are two more important things to do. You need to set a schedule for paying the allowance, and you must be faithful in following through.

Method of Payment

First, you need to set a regular payment schedule. You can pay your child's allowance weekly, biweekly (every two weeks), or monthly — whichever is easiest for you. Also, consider what payment schedule is best for her. Some twelve-year-olds and young teens may do better getting paid weekly or biweekly. Older teenagers should be capable of managing biweekly or monthly payments. Monthly payments are convenient because you can simply write her a check when you sit down to pay the monthly bills.

Be sure to tell her when she will be paid. It can be every Saturday at breakfast or every other Saturday. Maybe Sunday evening is good, or you can set payment for the first day of the month or the fifteenth. It can be any time you set, so make it for a time that suits your household schedule.

Secondly, you need to be reliable in paying her at this time. Just as you rely on picking up your paycheck at a certain time, she will rely on getting her allowance from you. If you want this system to be a success, don't skip any allowance payments. Be consistent.

Why is setting a schedule and having a specific time for payment important? 11Well, it trains her not to badger you for money at inopportune times. She knows when her payday is, and she has to wait until that date.

A schedule also discourages impulse buying. If there's an item she really wants to buy, but she has to wait several days before her allowance is paid, she'll have time to reconsider her purchase. Often, the desire to buy an item passes after a few days.

Should you pay her with cash or a check? This will depend on how often you are paying her and how mature she is. Cash is easier for preteens and young teens to manage. If she is an older teen and has easy access to a bank, a check can be beneficial. It is not as liquid as cash, so it might help her cut down on impulse spending.

In addition, getting her acquainted with bank services at this age is valuable. A visit to the bank to cash her check gives her the opportunity to deposit money in her savings account. At the same time, she'll see signs and banners for products the bank is offering, like free checking accounts and CDs. While she may not use these services now, at least she'll be aware of them, and she'll store the information away for later.

Should She Have a Checking Account?

As she gets older, she may find it handy to have her own checking account in which to deposit her monthly allowance. If she is under age eighteen, she can have an account with you as a co-signer. This is convenient because high school days seem peppered with costs for clothing purchases, application fees, yearbooks, gas, senior pictures, team photos, entrance exams, and the like. Even if you intend to cover some of these costs for her, it's easier if she can write a check and take care of these things at the time. You can simply reimburse her later.

Two of our children had checking accounts toward the end of their high school days. We took a few minutes with them and explained how checking accounts work. We emphasized keeping good records of the checks they'd written so they would know their balances. We warned about bouncing checks and never giving anyone a signed blank check. Showing them how to balance their checking accounts while they were still under our roof paid dividends (pun intended). We felt it was good practice before they went off to college.

It's easy to keep this allowance system on track if you set a regular payment time and follow through on paying them at that time. In addition to the other benefits of the system, if they put the money in a savings or checking account, they become acquainted with other banking services. Each positive result of the system builds on the others.

¢ *Pay allowances regularly by check or cash*

¢ *Explain how checking accounts work before they leave home*

Chapter 13

Sports and Enrichment

As I mentioned earlier in the book, sports and enrichment for children deserve special consideration. Given the importance of these activities in your child's social and intellectual growth, you may not want him or her subject to the ups and downs of the monetary learning process. You may also want to exercise a little more control over these areas to guarantee that they are not neglected. Then again, if there are conflicts over regular attendance at practice or the type and frequency of enrichment activities, you can solve those conflicts with the plan the way you did the shopping struggles. Either way you choose, think very carefully about whether or not to include the cost of sports and enrichment in the money you give your child each month.

Sports Fees

Most parents want to nurture their child's participation in sports. If your child has an interest in sports, you might not want to risk discouraging his participation by hanging it up on money issues.

Say you included sports fees in his allowance. A situation could develop in which your child opts to buy an expensive gadget rather than pay the twenty-dollar registration fee for soccer. You are then faced with the problem of seeing one purchase keep your child from an entire season of healthy sporting activity. Paying the fees yourself allows you to avoid such situations.

Another benefit of paying sporting fees yourself is the message it sends. Your child will know that you consider sports an important part of his growth. It may also signal another level of your participation in an activity that may be very important to him.

If you weigh the issues involved and decide that there is a compelling reason to include sports fees in your child's allowance amount, consider building in some elements of parental control, the way parents did in the examples I've given you in the sections on savings. And don't forget the reminders about fee deadlines.

Some parents negotiate a plan with their children that involves both sides paying a part of the fees. This may be especially effective for sports such as skiing or horseback riding, which involve more than a one-time fee.

For example, our children loved downhill skiing, but the cost of a couple of lift tickets wiped out their monthly allowances. We negotiated with them and agreed to pay for three lift tickets per ski season per child. They were responsible for paying for any additional trips themselves out of their regular allowances, or they could do extra jobs for us and earn money for more ski days.

Sports Equipment

If your child is involved in sports, he will need proper safety equipment, such as helmets, shin guards, goggles, and mouth guards. The few dollars you spend now on good equipment can save hundreds of dollars in medical bills later. I suggest you keep the ball in your court on this one. Buy the safety equipment for him. Let him kick in if he wants the latest fashion brand or super decals to dress up the equipment, but don't take any chances on the basic equipment.

Enrichment

Music, art, theater, dance, club activities, and social groups also play an important role in growing up. Because they are so vital to your child's healthy development, you may want to take financial control to ensure that these activities are included and that they continue. A budding musician should not quit taking lessons because he thought it good judgment to treat some friends to pizza rather than pay for his piano lessons. And if your aspiring actor fails to save the cost of his costume, he won't be the only one to suffer. The rest of the cast needs his costume to be ready too.

Recognizing the potential problems if the money is not there, some parents pay for lessons outright. Others ask their child to work to pay for part or all of the cost, believing the child cares more about lessons in which he has an investment. Whatever your financial means and family philosophy, you may want to retain some control over the spending decisions here to be certain that the doors of enrichment remain open for your child.

Control follows the money. If there is some budget item, such as sports and enrichment, that you feel more comfortable having under your control, don't include it in your child's monthly allowance. As he grows up and takes on more responsibility, you might consider including such items then.

¢ *Decide if you want to include the cost for sports in your child's allowance*

¢ *Cover the cost of sports safety equipment yourself*

¢ *Determine who covers the cost for lessons such as piano, karate, and ballet*

Chapter 14

A Dose of Reality

Most children are excited about starting on this allowance system. They look forward to the large sum of money each month and the opportunity to be in charge of their own spending choices. Some may be a little apprehensive because they recognize that the responsibility will be large as well, yet they are usually ready to charge forward.

Despite their best intentions, most of them spend their money very quickly at first. They are truly amazed that it's all gone in a couple of weeks. They find themselves with "too much month at the end of the money." To avoid discouragement in these initial months, you may need to exhibit some creative flexibility.

Becky and her friends had been planning for weeks to see the latest blockbuster horror movie. For weeks the television ads had been tantalizing potential viewers with frightening previews. Becky and her friends talked excitedly at lunch about which one of them would be scared the most. Rumors flew about the length of the box office lines.

On Friday of the movie's opening week, Becky grabbed her wallet and rushed for the door. She took one final, quick look to be certain the money was there. She stopped short. There was not enough money. With a sinking feeling she reviewed her last few purchases: the lunch with her friends, the clothes at the mall. She had carelessly failed to save out enough. Angrily, she berated herself under her breath. She knew that movie tickets were included in her monthly allowance now. What would she tell her friends, who were, at this very moment, waiting for her? She felt a rush of embarrassment. Thinking quickly, she rushed upstairs to her little brother's room.

"Mooooom! Becky says I have to give her my money because she didn't save any for the movies!"

"I did not! I only asked for a loan, Mom. I know it's my own fault. I wasn't careful enough, but EVERYBODY's going to see the movie tonight. We've been planning this for so long! I never said he had to give it to me."

Seeing Becky holding back the tears, her mom was sympathetic. She put her arms around Becky and gave her a reassuring hug.

"We all blow it sometimes. And I know how important tonight is to you. I'll tell you what. I'm going to give you five dollars for your ticket. But . . . you'll either have to earn it with some window washing this weekend, or you can take it as a loan from next month's allowance."

"Thanks, Mom. You're the best."

"And honey, you know how I'm into this 'learn your lesson' thing?"

"Yeah," Becky responded with an embarrassed smile.

"Don't assume a rescue next time, okay?"

"Okay."

Becky never complained when her next allowance was five dollars less than usual.

Was Becky's mom changing the rules here by advancing her daughter money? No, she was just helping her young teen to transition into a new system. She didn't become angry at her daughter. Instead, she gently coaxed her along to being a better money manager. It was a good compromise.

If Becky had the same problem in the next few months, should her mom bail her out again? Probably not. This time the answer from Mom should be, "Well, you've got to learn to plan ahead a little more."

Regular borrowing against the next month's allowance should be discouraged. Many of us know firsthand the dangers of making debt a lifestyle. You can, however, be flexible as you help your children through the transition period onto this system. For some children, this could take several months. But if you gently but firmly hold the line, they will learn to live within their allowance's limits. This is, after all, what you are trying to achieve.

It's Okay to Give Pointers

Don't be shy about giving advice when your child first goes on this system. At age twelve and thirteen, she hasn't had much training in planning ahead. You can help her by pointing out what items you foresee she will need in the next few months. If summer is coming, remind her she may need to buy a new bathing suit, sandals, shorts, and so on. If winter is approaching, remind her that last year's coat may not fit this season. You can give her a little prodding but still not be involved in her spending decisions. Soon, she will start to get the hang of planning ahead. She'll start to think more about her purchases. She will begin to develop good life skills for managing her money.

Praise Can Do Wonders

Probably the best way to support her is to keep a positive attitude about her abilities. Remaining supportive can do far more to steer her toward making smart purchases than any grumbling you do.

Simple comments like, "I really like that shirt you bought. I bet you'll get a lot of wear out of it," will reinforce that she's doing a good job in spending her money. Or you might say, "You were smart to buy that jacket a little big. It'll serve you well while you're still growing." If you take just two seconds to praise her when she shows good judgment, you'll see her making more and more good moves.

As further encouragement, six months to a year after she has settled into this system, you can give her "incentive pay," if your budget allows. Just as good workers receive incentive pay, a responsible child can get raises. It doesn't have to be a lot of money. Even a couple of dollars more per month will tell her how much you appreciate the grown-up manner in which she is handling her allowance. She'll love your approval.

Need Some Time to Grow Up?

What if you put her on this system, and she is not coping well? What if she is consistently irresponsible with the money? What if she is reckless and is not taking care of her needs?

Then you may need to take charge and discontinue the system. Tell her she can try it again in about six months or a year. Without yelling and blaming her, simply tell her that it was probably a little too much responsibility for her to handle at her age. Just let her grow up a little more, and soon she'll probably be quizzing you about when she can go back on the system. A day will come when she will really want to manage her own money.

The Quiet Ones

You should be aware that you may have a child who is on the other end of the spectrum. She appears totally responsible and rarely voices any concerns about the money. She manages whatever amount you give her without a peep.

This is great, but be sure to ask her periodically, "How are you getting along? Do you like being on this system? Do you want to continue on it?" Always keep the door for discussion open. You don't want her stressed about the money without you knowing it and being able to help.

If you feel it's too much pressure for her, offer to take her off the system. She may not be ready to handle this responsibility now, but sometime in the teen years she'll definitely want control of the purse strings. That's when she'll be ready to benefit from the system and learn the value of money.

Moving on up

When your children start on the large allowance amount, they really begin learning the value of a dollar. They will make some unwise purchases, but this is a good way to give them a dose of reality. Like Becky, they may spend the bulk of their allowance money on clothes and then have no money for their movie ticket. Your job, at this time, is to support them and encourage them to plan ahead.

Suggest they write down their income, including the allowance, any gift money, and money from part-time jobs. Help them list what they think their financial needs are for the next few weeks. This planning helps them monitor their spending so they don't run out of money all the time.

Talk, the Bottom Line

You want this system to be a success, so keep the lines of communication open with your kids, especially in the first few months. If they perceive that you are in the wings ready to give pointers when they ask, they'll get through this reality check much easier. By far, the best way to support them during this steep learning curve is to praise them when they show good judgment with their money. Talk may be cheap, but it can also be invaluable.

¢ *Be patient and supportive as they learn reality about the value of a dollar*

¢ *Give pointers to help them plan purchases*

¢ *Praise them when they make wise decisions about spending*

¢ *Consider giving them incentive pay*

¢ *Recognize if they are not ready for this responsibility yet*

¢ *Keep tabs on how they are coping*

¢ *Suggest they list their income and short-term needs*

¢ *Keep the lines of communication open*

Chapter 15

Clothing Tips to Help Your Teen's Budget

When it comes to clothes and teenagers, there are a few issues you will need to sort out. As always, take into consideration your child's individuality, your family's values, the lessons you want to teach, and the particular circumstances, and then come up with a response that you feel is appropriate.

First of all, if your children are responsible for buying all of their clothing with this allowance money, you may notice a gradual aging of items like socks and underwear. They tend to be low-priority items. As one dad said, "The clothing allowance system was great, but I couldn't stand how grubby my son's socks and underwear were getting. He just didn't want to spend any money on them." This dad solved the problem by buying the economical warehouse twelve-packs of socks and underwear for his son. Occasionally, he tempered the purchase by giving it to his son as an "early Christmas" or "early birthday" present. At other times, he just plain bought socks and underwear for his son to make himself feel better.

Another parent felt that her son would buy the jeans and T-shirts necessary for everyday wear, but he probably wouldn't buy dress slacks, shirts, and shoes for those occasions when he needed to be dressed up. Her solution was to hold back enough money from his clothing allowance each year to provide him with one dress-up outfit for church, weddings, and the like.

A second clothing crisis that parents of teens often face is the need now and then for prom dresses and tuxedos. High school proms are important events for many teens, and they involve considerable expense for both boys and girls. Clothing is only one of those costs. It would be good to decide in advance how to pay for these social events. Some parents exclude prom costs from the allowance system and expect to pay the bill themselves. Other parents agree to pay for half the cost of the evening. Don't forget to give your teen gentle reminders about saving for the prom if he is paying part of the cost.

To alleviate some of these prom costs, some innovative communities have established "prom closets" in their high schools that contain donated prom dresses that students can borrow for the evening. Usually the only money involved is for dry cleaning the dress before it is returned.

And for the tuxedos, don't forget to check the Salvation Army, Goodwill, Purple Heart, and other thrift stores. You might be surprised to find a tuxedo that fits with a little room to spare. Because tuxedos are not everyday wear, a used one can be in very good condition. It could be much cheaper to buy a used tuxedo than to rent one, especially if you have more than one teen who will need it.

A third potential trouble spot to watch out for is the teen version of "keeping up with the Joneses." With teens, that usually means clothing styles. In trying to keep up with what everyone else is wearing in this "clothing scene," your teen can end up making frivolous purchases with the money in hand. She may come home with an expensive turquoise and pink sweater that doesn't match any of her other clothes. She ends up, like many teens, wearing 20% of her clothes 80% of the time while the sweater gathers dust in the top of the closet.

Here's how one family helped its teenager get a grip on her wardrobe:

Kathy had a closet full of clothes, most of which she had purchased herself. She stood in the open door of the closet, as she had many times before, and groaned, "I have nothing to wear!" Instead of responding with the stereotypical parent retort, "What do you mean? You have lots of clothes," Kathy's mom understood what Kathy meant: she had no clothes that she liked on herself.

"I've got an idea," said Mom. "Kathy's birthday is coming up. Why don't we all pool our money and get her some clothing advice?" With the help of birthday money from Grandma and Grandpa (who never knew what to buy their teenage granddaughter), the family presented Kathy with a gift certificate for a professional fashion consultation.

With the advice of the professional, who treated her like a fashion model, Kathy learned what styles and colors looked best on her. She even got some makeup tips to go with her new awareness of clothing style. Not only did she begin to shop wiser, she began to receive compliments on what she was wearing.

With a little creative thinking, this wise mother helped her daughter with her wardrobe, her self-esteem, her budget, and her knowledge of fashion, a skill that would serve her well as she entered the working world.

If the prices for consultations are too high, you can check the bookstores for an appropriate book on the subject. Learning to coordinate a wardrobe can save lots of money in clothing purchases over the years.

Finally, if you have a boy, there's probably going to be an occasion during his teen years when he will need to don a suit jacket. "Oh, great," you think, "if I buy one, he'll probably wear it once or twice before he outgrows it." Time for some creative problem solving!

Here's how one high school boy took care of the suit jacket problem and helped out his buddies at the same time:

Jim came home from school one Friday afternoon and informed his mother he was going to be crowned Homecoming King at the high school dance that night. It was customary for the King to wear a suit jacket and tie to escort the Homecoming Queen. Since clothes were Jim's responsibility in his monthly allowance, and since he hadn't planned ahead on the suit jacket item, he said, "I'm going down to the thrift shop and see what I can find."

He returned wearing a beautiful wool blend jacket that looked first quality. "How do you like it, Mom? I got it for only $10. It's a little big, but that's okay 'cause I figure I'm going to grow some more."

She glanced up and saw him showing off his purchase.

It was bright red.

He wore the red jacket proudly to the dance, although his friends all razzed him about it. Soon one of his friends needed a jacket for a dress-up occasion and asked Jim if he could borrow his. During Jim's high school days, most of his friends borrowed the jacket for one occasion or another. When one of them said, "I'm going over to Jim's to borrow The Jacket," they all knew what he meant.

So, before you rush out to buy a suit jacket for one special event, check with your friends and neighbors. There may be a "Jacket" floating around out there that you can borrow.

Whether it's underwear, prom dresses, tuxedos or suit jackets, you can decide what clothing items, if any, you want to pay for. And don't be afraid to be creative.

¢ *Pay for clothing items you want to keep under your control*

¢ *Decide who pays for clothes for special events such as proms*

¢ *Give a wardrobe consultation to teens caught up in the "clothing scene"*

¢ *Check with friends to borrow clothing items for one-time occasions*

Chapter 16

How Can You Combat Commercialism and Peer Pressure?

Surveys say that the average household has the TV on for 7 1/2 hours each day. If this is true for your household, your children are bombarded with 400 commercials per week.

As early as age three or four, you can intervene and soften the impact of these commercials by explaining to your children that a company is trying to sell them a product. Tell them that the product may not be as good as it sounds. Remind them as often as you can to be wary of the hype. If you do this, they'll grow up with a healthy skepticism about products that are pitched at them. They'll learn to see through the advertising publicity.

You can still let them make purchasing decisions about products seen on television, but preface the decision with comments like, "Maybe you should see the product yourself and then decide if you think it's worth buying." Often, when children see the real thing, it's not what they expected, and they won't buy it.

Television, magazine, and billboard advertising are hard enough to combat. Children also get caught up in peer pressure. Before you stress too much about it, recognize that it's just a natural part of growing up and belonging. They want to be like their friends and have what their friends have. All the parental ranting in the world won't stop them from going through this very natural stage. But you can help set some guidelines.

When the peer pressure hits and they want all sorts of material goods, take a few minutes to encourage them to think about their purchases. If everyone's wearing purple tennis shoes with pink stripes, and they really want a pair, you might try this approach. Instead of saying an outright "no," tell them you'd like them to wait a few days. If they still want the purple tennis shoes, tell them you will buy them next weekend. This helps curb impulse spending. They might still get the purple tennis shoes, but they'll have had a few days to plan the purchase. Small lessons in consumerism are being taught here.

When they are teenagers and you turn the spending choices for clothes and shoes over to them, they'll have the responsibility for the decision of what to buy. When it's their money and there's a set amount for the month, purple-and-pink tennis shoes may not be high on their list for very long. They may really want them, but their available money supply will start them thinking about whether they really "need" them. Just sit back and watch the magic happen.

Just a few minutes a day talking to your children about TV commercials when they are young will help them discern the hype and make them wiser consumers. You can still expect them to get caught up in peer pressure to buy items, but perhaps not quite as much if you've taught them to perceive advertising for what it is.

Advertising aimed at kids today is not just to sell toys, clothes, and shoes. Food and grocery products now flood the kids' market. And it's not just cereal products that are offered. Kids' versions of cheese sauces, french fries, yogurt, salad dressings, chicken nuggets, graham crackers, and oatmeal are popular.

Who's buying all this stuff? Parents and kids are. Parents are indulging their children more, and kids, who are doing more of the grocery shopping these days, are a captive audience.

Unfortunately, nutritional content has taken a back seat in many of these products. They appeal to kids but they're loaded with fat, sugar, and artificial coloring. Kids who spend their allowance money on them are getting shortchanged.

¢ *Explain commercials to your child at a young age*

¢ *Don't stress over peer pressure to buy material goods — this system monitors it for you*

Chapter 17

Some Gray Areas

Just when you think you've got all the bases covered about who is responsible for paying for what, some gray areas may come up. Most can be solved on an individual basis and need not be a problem. More complex gray areas and issues about money rear their heads in the teenage years, so you need to prepare for how to handle them.

Special Treats

The first gray area involves special treats. Let's say you've had your daughter on this system for several months. She is doing a pretty good job of learning how to manage her allowance money and seems to be covering her needs.

You're out enjoying a shopping day at the mall with her and you see her admiring an outfit. She'd love to have it for the school dance Friday night, but she doesn't have enough money left in her clothing allowance to buy it. You've got some extra cash. Should you indulge her and buy it for her?

As parents, we get a lot of pleasure from occasionally buying treats for our children, such as clothing for special events. If you feel your daughter would view this purchase as a special treat from you, go ahead and enjoy yourself and buy it for her. She will have plenty of other items to budget on a regular basis to learn money management. An occasional deviation from this system will do no harm. Just don't do it so often that she expects you to treat her every time you go shopping. Make indulgences the exception rather than the rule.

"Unplanned Opportunities"

In addition to enrichment activities such as guitar lessons, art classes, and field trips, there will be what I like to call "unplanned opportunities" that fall into the gray area. They will surely come up, and they cost money. Some of the opportunities may not be that important to your child, and she'll let go of them easily; other opportunities can become a source of friction, especially during the teenage years. First, here's an easy one to solve:

> You've just gotten home from work and your thirteen-year-old son has been waiting for you.
> "Hey, Dad, guess what! Our baseball team's going to see the Giants play the Dodgers on Saturday. I've always wanted to see them play. Everyone's going! Can I go? Do I have to pay for this out of my allowance money? Can I buy lunch there?"
> He's a big baseball fan, and you know it will be a thrill for him to go with his team. Finances permitting, you can give him the money for his ticket and hot dog, or split the cost with him.

Here's a harder "opportunity" to solve that involves your fifteen-year-old daughter:

> She's been on the junior varsity volleyball team at high school and has potential for making varsity next year.
> "Mom! I'm sooo excited," she exclaims. "Our varsity team is going to the playoffs in Los Angeles. It's an overnight trip and there's a few

seats left on the bus. It's $80 for a hotel room and food. Can you sign this permission slip?"

This is another gray area because the costs for motels and meals weren't plugged into her charts when figuring her monthly allowance. They are unforeseen items. With teenagers, you can not only expect the unexpected, but you can expect that the costs go up for everything and, of course, the issues get harder to sort out. As they get older, you will need to evaluate these occasional requests for money that weren't plugged into their regular allowance.

For a situation like this volleyball tournament, a good guideline is to ask yourself, "Is this an opportunity out of the ordinary that my child won't otherwise have the privilege of attending? Will it enhance and enrich her?" If you think so, and you can afford it, go ahead and pay her way, or pay for part of it. Or, you can give her a loan to cover the cost. She'll know it's a special event that you think is important. Once again, treating them to occasional events won't erode the lessons you're trying to teach in this allowance system.

Cultural Choices

In the course of their growing up, your teenagers will be exposed to a whole array of cultural choices. You may find yourself in this situation:

Your teenage son wants to attend a rock concert that's a three-hour drive away. His newly licensed friend is driving and they won't get home until around three in the morning. You think the rock group is a bad influence. You don't like their music, and you especially dislike their style.

"I really want to go," he pleads. "But tickets are $40 each, and I only have about $10 right now. Can I have $30 so I can go?"

Now you're into some harder issues. If your main concern is your son's personal safety because of the young driver and the scene at the concert, tell him he can't go. And if you are adamantly opposed to the messages generated by this rock group, tell him you don't want him to go. But let's say everything is safe, and your only true opposition is that it's not the type of music you enjoy. You have to recognize when you are imposing your own cultural choices on him. Obviously, he likes this kind of music. Are you going to use money to control his cultural choice?

If you don't feel right in controlling his choice with money, a good response might be to loan him thirty dollars. This way, he'll be paying for the whole ticket and you won't be dictating his choices. He is able to go to the concert, yet you haven't condoned it by paying his way.

Some of my own teenagers' cultural choices were not to my liking. However, I knew if I forbade them to attend, I would be driving a wedge between us. Generally, I would say, "Okay, I'm going to give you this loan." Then, looking them directly in the eyes, I would add, "You can go, but I'd rather you didn't." I stated my opposition, but in a non-confrontational way.

There is a flip side to this attempt to control choices. Suppose the world famous cellist Yo Yo Ma is performing in your city. You think it's an opportunity not to be missed. You're waving the money for tickets in your children's faces, but they don't want to go. Again, you're trying to use money to impose your cultural choice on them. Be careful. They may hear the message, "The rules of this allowance plan only apply to my choices, not theirs." Kids are masters at sniffing out any hint of hypocrisy.

Despite the planning and the charts, unexpected situations — gray areas — will pop up. It's impossible to foresee them, so just deal with them on an individual basis, remembering your own values and the principles underlying this plan.

¢ *Enjoy buying occasional treats for your children — it won't erode your allowance system*

¢ *Deal with "unplanned opportunities" on an individual basis*

¢ *Determine how you will handle cultural choices*

Chapter 18

The Complaint Department Is Now Open

Any effective learning process is fraught with struggles and stress. With something as sophisticated as money management, you should expect your kids to feel the pressure at times. It is at such times that you will hear that oh-so-common method of dealing with frustration and uncertainty: the complaint.

After being on the system for three months, our twelve-year-old daughter was having problems.

"I don't think I have enough allowance money," she began. "I had to pay eight dollars for the bus for the science class field trip, and I had to buy white tennis shoes for the gym show. And I had to get a birthday present for Angie and, you know, Grandma's birthday is coming up, and pretty soon I'll have to think about Christmas presents . . ."

We made her monthly allowance payments to her on the first of the month, and she was reciting this tale of woe on the twelfth. She was running out of money even before the middle of the month.

We listened to her complaint and reminded her that she had agreed that the allowance was realistic when we filled in the chart. We also quizzed her a bit on where she had spent her money. She accounted for some of the money, but the purchases she recited did not add up to the whole allowance.

We didn't refuse to give her a raise, nor did we hand her more money. Instead, we asked her to keep a record of all her spending for the next two months. In order to justify giving her more allowance, we needed to see how she was spending the money. So, for the next two months, she documented almost every cent she spent. This was difficult for a twelve-year-old, but she was intent on proving that she needed more money.

At the end of the two months, we sat down and went over her expenses. It turned out that she had spent a lot on ice cream, candy, and junk food, not just for herself, but also for friends. In addition, she purchased some pretty expensive gifts for her friends' birthdays.

We complimented her generosity but also suggested that she needed to tone it down. She agreed that maybe there were some areas where she could cut back. We urged her to try this and to keep better tabs on her spending.

Over the next few months she came home from school and munched on apples and carrots more often, and, with our coaching, she set a ten dollar limit on birthday gifts for friends. She began to take more notice of her spending habits, and after a few months she got along nicely on her allotted amount. She even started telling her friends what a "neat" allowance system it was.

So, when you hear complaints about the amount of allowance — and you probably will — don't rush to give your children more money or to take them off the system. They are merely learning how to be good consumers. It's beneficial for them to go through this process of voicing their objections. By speaking up, they can learn. And they do you a favor by pinpointing trouble spots.

How to Handle Chronic Complainers

What if you have a child who complains month after month that the allowance amount is not enough? What if you've asked him to document his spending and he can't account for all of it? Or, maybe he doesn't want to admit that he's spending a lot on video games, doughnuts, and fast food.

Once again, remind him that he agreed to the amount as realistic at the start. He may try to convince you that the allowance is below the national poverty level, but you know better.

You have several options here:

1) Review the charts. You might agree he needs a slight increase.
2) Hold the line and tell him he has to manage the amount given. Agree to review his budget with him in six months.
3) Suggest he get a part-time job to supplement his allowance.

Working Part-time Can End the Complaints

A few hours spent delivering newspapers, mowing lawns, or babysitting will get him away from television and won't affect homework time. If he really wants more money, he'll be willing to get a job. If your budget allows, you can hire him yourself to clean out the garage, wash windows, wash the car, or vacuum and dust.

If your budget is stretched and you can't afford to pay him any more, take time to explain the realities of your financial limits. Share with him that you're on a monthly budget too, and that you are working hard to cover the bases. That's why you're suggesting he get a part-time job. If we give our kids rational reasons for what we decide, they most often respond with rational reactions.

In summary, hearing some complaints about the amount of money can be music to your ears. Think of complaints as the sounds of learning. It's how they voice their uncertainty. Your children are beginning to learn how to manage their money. They will need a minimum of six months to adjust to their new spending privileges. Don't be surprised if some of them take much longer. Give them the time they need. The beginning stages of acquiring money management skills is crucial. Their sound money education is your goal, so be patient.

¢ *Expect complaints about the allowance amount during the start-up months*

¢ *Give options to chronic complainers*

¢ *Suggest they get a part-time job*

Chapter 19

Should We Buy Our Kids a Car?

When it comes to cars and teenagers, one fact is certain: most teenagers want one. Most other aspects of this issue are debatable. Is teen car ownership important? Is it wise? Who should pay? Who provides the money for oil, gas, insurance, and maintenance? As with college costs, different parents and teenagers use different strategies for coping with car ownership.

One couple had no intentions of providing cars for their children. Instead, they provided each of their teenagers with a gas credit card and told them to be generous in filling up their friends' gas tanks. They knew the monthly gas bills would be considerably cheaper than car payments and insurance if their children had cars.

The other end of the spectrum was the dad who bought his son a brand new car to drive to college. This dad knew his son was a level-headed young man. He preferred to have his son behind the wheel, rather than having him be a passenger in the car of another, not-so-responsible teenager. His motivation for buying the car was mainly safety.

In between these two philosophies are many of us who share our family cars with our teenagers, help them buy cars of their own, or make them car loans. If you're wondering how to make the decision about a car, you can use the "want" versus "need" distinction. Do your teenagers "want" or "need" a car? If they can conveniently get to school, jobs, lessons, and sports without driving, you're probably looking at a "want." If a car would really lessen the burden of getting them to school, jobs, lessons, and sports, then you're probably looking at a "need."

While this is a good guideline, it's only a beginning. It doesn't address all of the issues involved. Peer pressure, freedom and independence are also strong incentives for teens to get cars. Though parents often worry about this increased freedom, the accompanying responsibility can be a good experience and balance out the potential negatives. One of our children came up with a plan to get her "own wheels" when she was seventeen.

Beginning in early high school, she had a part-time job clerking and doing bookkeeping in a sporting goods store that paid better than minimum wage, and she had a nice little sum in savings. Since she had a regular income, she asked if she could have the sum total of her future allowance payments through high school graduation. With this money and her savings, she could buy a used car. She assured us she would cover her clothing, gas, insurance, lunches, gifts, entertainment, and the like from her paycheck. She really wanted a car, and since we weren't going to buy her one, we agreed to advance her the lump sum. We had reservations, but we admired her work ethic and innovation. It turned out she had to work some weekends, in addition to her weekday hours, to cover her expenses, but she pulled it off and never regretted buying the car.

Whether your teenagers have their own car or share the family car, they will appreciate the privilege more if they have to cover some of the costs. Their contribution could range from buying an occasional tank of gas and helping with the cost of additional insurance, to paying for everything themselves. The more financial support they provide, the less they will take this transportation for granted.

Here's how one generous dad looked beyond his children's teenage years regarding cars. He knew that when his children entered the work force, there would probably be a true necessity for them to own cars. As each child came to that crossroads, he offered a loan for a dependable used car that would help in launching into a career. The repayment schedule and interest charges began six months after each child started work. These children were lucky because this "Bank of Dad" had low interest rates.

You can't blame teenagers for wanting a car. They've grown up watching us love our automobiles. The bottom line about whether they have a car will mainly be determined by your finances and theirs. Generally, teens who contribute to the initial cost of a car and who pay a portion of the ongoing expenses will take better care of it and will appreciate its benefits more.

¢ *Understand that buying a car is followed by ongoing expenses*

¢ *Know that teenagers want cars for a variety of reasons*

¢ *Discuss your feelings about cars with them*

¢ *Suggest they share in the cost*

Chapter 20

Should My Child Have a Credit Card?

We are surrounded by plastic these days. Credit card companies use aggressive marketing campaigns, touting giveaways and promotions, to seduce us into using their cards. It's easy for young adults to be lured by these marketing techniques. It used to be that we only used credit when we had to borrow money. Today, we use credit cards as part of daily life. For this reason, it's important that you have a heart-to-heart talk with your children about the convenience of credit cards, along with the perils.

You should explain that some credit card companies charge annual fees, along with interest on the unpaid balance. If your children chalk up big balances and pay just the minimum payment each month, it can take years to pay off the debt, and it costs them big bucks in interest charges. Tell your children that credit cards can be very convenient, but they must be careful not to overuse them. Remember, children learn by example, so prudent use of your own credit cards is their first, best teacher.

Some credit card companies offer "student cards" that have lower credit limits than regular credit cards and require parents to co-sign with the child. With such an arrangement, if your child can't make the payments, you are responsible. Despite the risk to your budget, this can be a valuable tool for introducing your child to credit while giving you an automatic connection to the choices.

Debit cards or "secured cards" are another way to teach teenagers how to limit the use of credit. A deposit is made to an account, and your teen can then charge on this account. Using the card is just like writing a check against this account. The amount teenagers can charge, however, is determined by the limit in their account. This system can be a valuable stepping stone to a regular charge card. Some parents feel better if their children have a credit card available when they leave home for jobs, travel, or college. The card gives them an option in emergencies. Here's how one parent handled the credit card issue when her children left for college:

> For convenience's sake, she added her children's names to her credit card. She impressed upon them that this card was a privilege and could only be used for emergencies and necessary college bookstore purchases such as textbooks, notebooks, lab materials, and computer software. Each month she checked her statements to verify purchases. She slept better knowing they had this safety net in case of emergency. If any of them thought an "emergency" was to charge $50 rock concert tickets, his name would be removed from the credit card, and he would owe her for the charge.
>
> She explained to them the exact use of the card and told them she expected to pay off the balance every month to avoid interest charges. Toward the end of college, she suggested the children apply for their own credit cards because she intended to remove their names from hers.

This plan proved to be an efficient way for her children to purchase their necessary materials while learning about credit. None of them abused the credit card because she had "lectured" them before adding their names to it. When initiating such a plan, it's also a good idea to remind your children that credit is going to be valuable to them as young adults. They will need good credit ratings when buying their first car or renting an apartment, so a clean slate is important.

Whatever approach you take with credit cards, be sure to explain to your children how they work before they leave home. Otherwise, they can be one convenience that gets children in a lot of debt if no one has explained their proper use.

¢ *Talk to your children about credit cards* before *they leave home*

¢ *Start with a debit card or "secured card" as a stepping stone*

¢ *Add your children, if you desire, to your credit card for convenience and safety*

¢ *Remind children they will need a good credit record to buy cars and rent apartments*

Chapter 21

Instilling a Work Ethic

Good things come to those who work. Material rewards are the fruit of diligent labor. These are values as American as, well, apple pie. Back when most of us worked on the farm, whether picking apples or harvesting grain or tending the livestock, our children had a daily demonstration of the value of work and its connection to the rewards of food, shelter, clothing, and health.

Today, many children would be hard pressed just to describe the jobs their parents do for a living, let alone how that work is connected to the clothes they wear and the food they eat. Our daily bread comes from some bakery we've never seen, and the latest sweater was pulled off the shelf at Macy's, not Mother's loom. For those kids whose parents work at home, the connections may be a little easier to grasp, but for the vast majority of modern sons and daughters, those connections are obscure. So how do we teach our children a work ethic?

Creating the connections that are often clouded by the contemporary work scene is one of the wonderful benefits of this allowance system. Because the system starts in the home and is tied to the work the child does there, she can begin to see the connections between labor and reward in a small context. Eventually, the plan expands the boundaries beyond the home so that the child can carry the lessons learned into the larger world.

There are ways, however, that the carry-over of knowledge can be nudged along, ways to help your kids notice the connections to the larger world of work and pay. One such way is to create in your home a reflection of the work-a-day world.

Your At-Home Company

If you give your children an allowance on a regular basis in exchange for certain chores to be done, you are already teaching them a work ethic. If you want to be certain they transfer this ethic to their dealings outside the home, find the similarities between your system and the real corporate world and share them with your child. This will help them begin to understand the business world by relating it to what they know. The comparison also can serve to give your household system more credibility. Here are some examples of the kinds of connections you can make:

The company manager	Mom and/or Dad
The employees	The children
Company policy	The allowance plan
Job description	The list of required chores
Paycheck	Allowance
Benefits	Room and board

By referring to these comparisons, you can stress the importance of your allowance plan and the lessons your children are learning. At the same time, you are making the real job world less of a mystery to them. As a result, they can carry the work ethic from home out into the larger world with ease.

Of course, none of us would actually renege on providing room and board for our children or run our households in the detached manner often necessary in the business world, but the connections can still be very useful.

"But you didn't do your chores. No business will pay you if you don't do your work!"

"A company can't change its policies every time they are inconvenient for an employee."

"A company is not going to change your salary just because you need more money one month."

It never hurts to find new and creative ways to emphasize the lessons your kids are learning.

Value Received for Value Given

Another way to help kids better understand the work ethic they are learning is to pay them piecemeal at an early age. An hourly wage has little meaning for most young children; they learn to connect pay to the passing of time and not to the work. This could lead to procrastination as a work value. (You don't have an employer's option of termination.) We have already discussed paying your children by the job. To further emphasize the connection between labor and pay, you may consider paying some jobs (especially longer ones) by the item completed, that is, piecemeal.

In this method of payment, the child receives more pay the more work she completes. If you say to a young child, "I'll pay you one dollar an hour to pull dandelions from the lawn," your offer will mean little to her. If you say, "I'll pay you five dollars to pull the dandelions from the lawn," the offer will seem a little more real, but the connection between the actual pulling of a dandelion and the money will still be distant and a little vague.

Try saying, "I'll pay you a nickel for every dandelion you pull from the lawn." Suddenly, the pulling of each weed has a significant monetary meaning. The connection between work and pay is reinforced with each dandelion. Your child has a strong motivation to do a good job, that is, seek out every single dandelion and pull it. She also has a reason not to dawdle. The quicker she pulls, the higher the pile of dandelions and nickels. As children grow older and can make connections more easily, the piecemeal method is no longer necessary. They respond better to "per job" wages. This still works more efficiently than an hourly wage for reinforcing the work ethic.

Setting the Working Stage

In addition to helping your children make connections between their allowances and the business world, there are other things you can do to reinforce the work ethic at home. One of those is establishing a positive attitude toward the workplace.

Your children will already have a positive attitude toward their own "workplace," their home. It is a place where many wonderful things happen. Yet we can undermine the transfer of that attitude to the outside work world.

When things don't go right for us at work, we tend to come home and complain. It's good therapy to vent our frustrations, especially in a place that is safe, like home. But if we complain too often without balancing our comments with the positive things about our work, our children may start to look on the workplace as an unfriendly place to be. Why would they make an effort to join it as adults? If, on the other hand, you come home from work with success stories and enthusiasm for the day's labor, your children will more likely connect your workplace with theirs, a safe and good place. You can still relate the negative aspects of your job, just as you want them to be free to discuss their complaints at home, but you do so in an objective manner, balancing the negative and the positive. Your children will see your workplace as an exciting place to be, and they will associate a paycheck with a good quality of life. As always, in this you are your child's first teacher.

Seeing the World at Work

To reinforce the work ethic even more strongly, you can take your positive talk of work one step further: take your child to your place of employment.

There is a positive trend in many businesses that is encouraging parents to bring their kids to work on special days. Some businesses have an annual "bring your kids to work" day. Management understands the value of children connecting their businesses to a positive lifestyle. They are, after all, the future work force.

Going to work with Mom or Dad is a powerful bonding time for a child. It also helps her understand the parent's work in a more concrete way. She can see for herself that Dad works for his paycheck the same way she works for her allowance. Suddenly, the outside work environment is a very familiar place, full of rewards and future opportunities.

It does not need to stop there. You don't have to be limited by your own profession. Take time to expose your child to other workers by including her on your various appointments and errands when it's convenient.

We took our children to visit our lawyer's office when we signed our will. My husband and I had previously met with our lawyer to revise our will, so this visit was only for signing the finished document. We told the children they had to dress up (look presentable) because we wanted them to meet Mr. Phillips. We called him earlier to tell him we'd like to bring the family along as a way of giving our children glimpses at different professions. He was very gracious and made a big deal about shaking their hands and showing them his office. They sat in the cushy chairs, admired his huge mahogany desk, and took special notice of the wall-to-wall, leather-bound law books.

It doesn't always have to be a planned visit like this, or require an appointment. If you have business at the bank, for example, take them along and introduce them to the bank officer. If you're having a new muffler installed on the car, take a few minutes to let them watch the mechanic. If you have a repairman fixing a household appliance, encourage them to watch. A glimpse at a wide variety of occupations is valuable because you never know what might grab their attention. Instilling a work ethic in your children can begin with paying them an allowance for doing chores. Equating their chores to jobs in a real company is a simple way to explain work for pay. Piecemeal work and "per job" prices are great incentives for young workers. And remember to let them see not only yourself, but others at work in their jobs. The benefits of reinforcing the work ethic will last a lifetime.

¢ *Pay an allowance for chores to teach work for pay*

¢ *Teach value received for value given*

¢ *Make sure the stage you set at home is a positive one*

¢ *Let them see the world at work*

Chapter 22

Ages 18 to 22: Stepping into Independence

The first years of a child's adulthood can be a rewarding time for the parent who has labored to teach financial responsibility. That parent's job becomes one of fine-tuning the lessons learned and providing limited assistance. Mostly, it's a time of watching with reassurance your child's ability to handle the demands of the world outside of the nest.

Sometime between the ages of eighteen and twenty-two, you can phase out their allowance money. An exception to this might be those who are doing volunteer work or are in-training or college. If your children have moved completely out of your house, your days of dropping hints about money management are probably over (unless you're lucky, and they call you for advice). Essentially, you should be working toward an end to the allowance and the guidance. It's time for them to take full responsibility for themselves. You can welcome them to adulthood!

Paychecks Offer a Golden Opportunity to Save

For those young adults going to work full time, remind them to do the following:

1) Save money on a *regular* basis.
2) Pay themselves *first*.

No matter how small their paychecks, they should first take a little money off the top and deposit it in savings. Ten percent of their net earnings is a good target amount. If automatic payroll savings plans are available to them, they should take advantage of this service. By doing so, they can build a nice little nest egg in a short time.

Remind them, as often as you can without controversy, that it would be disappointing to let an entire first year's income slip through their fingers with nothing to show for their hard work. Hopefully, the savings habit will have been ingrained from a young age so you won't have to nag.

Your official years of coaching your children in money management are now coming to a close. Between the ages of eighteen and twenty-two, they should phase out of this system and take financial responsibility for themselves. This doesn't mean you stop talking about money. On the contrary, since money has always been something you discussed with them, they will probably feel comfortable asking you for advice.

Off to College

Instead of entering the work force, maybe your children are off to college. As a transition period into the working world, the college years will require a little more involvement on your part than if your child had gone immediately to work. Still, because of your past efforts in training your son or daughter, your part can be minimal.

We wanted our children to attend college so we started a savings program when they were young. By doing so, we had the advantage of long-term growth for the investment. In addition, our children had saved money for college in their Post-High School Funds (discussed in Chapter 9).

We agreed to pay room, board, tuition, and books for four years for each of our children. We stressed four years because it's costly to stretch college out over five to six years. We wanted our children to understand that our financial support for their education was not unlimited.

In exchange for the privilege of going to college, our children no longer received "the big money" every month. It was now their responsibility to cover their personal expenses for clothing, local transportation, gas, dating, fraternity/sorority fees, recreation, hobbies, and entertainment — in essence, any personal expenses beyond their room and board.

We made two exceptions to this:

1) transportation costs to come home (the number of trips was determined by distance and cost), and
2) telephone charges to keep in touch with brothers and sisters and to call home.

We agreed to cover transportation costs for them to come home because we wanted them around for holidays, and we wanted to keep in touch with them. We also agreed to pay for telephone charges to us and to siblings because we didn't want our good family rapport curbed by their budget restrictions. These expenditures benefited us as much as they did our kids.

At the start of college, they could begin to tap their Post-High School Funds to cover their personal, freshman-year expenses. This fund, as previously explained, was aimed at launching them into college with enough money so they wouldn't need a job during that first critical year.

Did it work? Yes, but differently for each child. One, who hadn't saved as much, ran through the money quickly and had to get a job before the end of the freshman year. Another one lasted nicely on the Post-High School Fund through freshman year and found a part-time job in the sophomore year. The third one had the advantage of a partial scholarship and, therefore, didn't need a part-time job until her junior year. All in all, the Post-High School Funds served them well during the college transition year. It was wonderful to watch the positive outcome of all those years of gentle reminders.

Scholarships

Sometimes our involvement in the first year was a little more direct. Our daughter who was offered a partial college scholarship had a big decision to make. She felt she should accept the money because it would alleviate our financial crunch, but she was not convinced she would fit in at the college that made the offer. We, of course, wanted to say, "Take it!," but we didn't want to dictate her college choice.

Instead, we came up with an incentive plan. We knew she had earned the academic scholarship by studying hard in high school. We offered her the equivalent of one-third of the scholarship money toward her personal expenses if she decided to attend that college. She thought it was a great offer and accepted. We then had the other two-thirds of the money to help cover her college costs. It was this extra money that kept her from needing a part-time job until her junior year of college. It was not only a financial plus for her and us, but she loved her college choice and fit right in. More rewards for our parental labor of love!

(By the way, scholarships should be applied for at every opportunity. But even if your children are not offered scholarships, keep in mind that colleges offer work-study programs, loans, and financial aid. They are in the business of producing graduates, and they want to retain students.)

Since we all have different financial bases, we need to negotiate college costs with our children. Generally, children who know they have to help the family pay for college will do more to accomplish this than parents expect.

If funds are limited, the community college level is a great place to start, with an eye toward transferring into a four-year college later. However, you could offer your children the choice of four years at a moderately priced college rather than the first two years paid at a more expensive campus where they would then have to get loans or work-study to pay for the last two years themselves.

In any case, it's best to start college savings plans for your children when they are young. Clearly, planning ahead alleviates some of the financial worries when your children turn eighteen. They, of course, are going to have to help with these costs, so urge them to visit their high school guidance and counseling offices to explore scholarship possibilities. Asking just a few questions can save them a great deal of financial stress in the future. Keep in mind the old adage, "Where there's a will, there's a way," and you will be able to map out a plan for college with your children.

For us, the early start really paid off, and we were able to limit our involvement and enjoy watching our children move ahead responsibly without us.

¢ *Phase out your allowance system*

¢ *Remind your children to save money regularly and to pay themselves first*

¢ *Cover college costs by beginning savings when your children are young*

¢ *Discontinue their monthly allowance when they start college*

¢ *Let them use the Post-High School Fund*

¢ *Apply for scholarships at every opportunity*

Chapter 23

Ten Good Reasons to Use This System

We've discussed how children will benefit from being on this system because it teaches day-to-day money management and boosts their self-esteem and confidence along the way. But you benefit, too. Here is my list of top ten reasons why you, as a parent, should want to use this system with your children:

(1) It keeps your own budget in line. You are not constantly doling out money whenever your children need or request it. You give them a set amount of allowance.

(2) It confirms that the money tree is indeed a myth. Your kids learn that your household does indeed run on a budget for a reason. A regular, set payment teaches children that planning is necessary. They learn there are limits on the amount of money available.

(3) It doesn't allow you to play favorites. It is equal for all children. You may have children of different ages on different allowance amounts, but you can assure the younger ones they will get the higher amount when they get older.
No longer will you hear complaints like, "You bought Susie three sweaters, and all I got

was socks." This is because the purchasing deci-sions your children make, beginning around junior high school age, are now their spending choices. They are the ones deciding whether to buy three sweaters or just a pair of socks. You are out of the decision.

This system is especially helpful for parents with blended families. Rather than Dad doling out allowance to "his" kids and Mom doling out allowance to "her" kids, a set amount (that is age appropriate) can be the standard to cover all kids.

4) It lets you share laundry tips with your kids. Our son purchased a red-and-white-striped rugby shirt using his clothing allowance money. At the first washing, it turned solid pink. He was angry and sad that he had spent his money on it. I encouraged him to take it back to the store. He did, and got a full refund. He learned an impor-tant lesson without my having to teach it, though I could take credit, of course.

I doubt he would have taken the time to return the shirt if it had been "my" money, not "his" money, that paid for it. The funny thing was that he began reading washing labels before he made future purchases. Not too many fourteen-year-olds read "Care Instructions" before plunk-ing down their money, but he did.

5) It amazes and amuses your friends. Children who make their own spending choices learn the real cost of goods. It doesn't take too many shopping trips before they take "their" money and head to the "On Sale" racks first. Merchandise on these sale racks becomes of great interest to them when it's "their" money and there's a limited amount.

A friend had her teenage son on this system and told me this story:

One afternoon during a meeting at her house, her son burst through the front door very excited. "Look what I found for $3!" he said, proudly holding up a pair of Bermuda shorts.

"Where did you get them?" she asked.

"At the Salvation Army Store," he beamed.

The assembled friends were stunned. My friend tried to play nonchalant, but no one in the meeting would continue until she explained how she got him to do that.

6) It cuts down on whining. Your children begin to distinguish between "want" and "need." They may "want" the latest styles, but do they "need" them? You are no longer involved in the decision. This month they may buy the expensive brand-name jeans, but in future months they'll begin to pace themselves on the pricey items.

7) It helps you track prices around town. Your kids become price informers. They learn comparison shopping. If they buy a video at one store and then see it cheaper at another store, they take notice. You can bet they'll compare prices on their next purchase.

8) It keeps your sewing machine primed. When one teenage girl saw the prices of prom dresses, she decided to make her dress. Not only did she save some money, but she had an "original" to wear to the prom. This, of course, is only one example of the kinds of creative action children take to work within their budgets.

9) It saves you from sounding tiresome and desperate by making vague comparisons to children in Third World countries. Children have a greater appreciation for the things they buy with their own money. On this system they have to plan ahead for purchases and figure out how much allowance money they have available. When money management falls in their court, their appreciation for the goods they buy increases.

10) Your children can now set goals for long-term purchases. Items like stereos, roller blades, computers, and bicycles are now a possibility for them to obtain. They know they have a set allowance coming on a regular basis, so it is easier for them to save up for big ticket items.

An added bonus is that children who save for months to purchase a big item like a bicycle, are going to take better care of it. It was not easy to get and they won't take it for granted.

Surprise Bonus Benefits: A Single Parent and a Child Support Problem

Some benefits of this system are almost impossible to anticipate. They arise from individual family circumstances.

One mom who had her daughter on this system used it to help solve a child support problem. A job promotion for her became available in a different city. She moved away with her fourteen-year-old daughter. Consequently, her daughter's contact with her dad became less frequent. Child support payments from her former husband became irregular. He was unhappy about their move and began questioning whether his payments were indeed supporting his daughter.

This mom understood his concerns and sent him a copy of their daughter's monthly expenses as determined from using the charts on pages 81 and 82. She told him their daughter now had her own checking account. If he wished, he could make the support checks out directly to his daughter who could deposit them in her own checking account.*

When he saw his daughter's list of monthly expenses and had the opportunity to send the checks directly to her, he responded by sending the payments faithfully. He also began including notes to her with each payment. She loved the notes and began writing back to him. It was a win-win situation.

¢ *Put the ten advantages of this system to work for you*

¢ *Be prepared for unanticipated benefits*

---

* If you are paying child support through an agency, check with the agency's rules on this.

Conclusion

It seems as if one day you are holding a vulnerable little baby, and the next you are watching her leave for her first full-time job. One minute he's crying in the delivery room, and the next he's shouting, "I got the job!" In the brief years between these milestones, we do our work as parents. We take those babies on a journey into adulthood. What a task. What an adventure!

There is so much to teach, so much to share. Money can easily get lost in the rush, especially when we as parents see it as boring, difficult, or distasteful. Yet money is like the middleman between our needs and desires and our satisfaction. It touches every aspect of our lives in some way. Learning to be in control of this powerful force in our lives is a big step toward happiness.

Teaching your children about money matters is not a cure-all for the troubles they will face. But good money skills can be a foundation upon which they can build a happy and productive life. Money becomes a tool, like a millstone that actually works to grind the wheat and not one that hangs around the neck.

One foresighted father summed up the learning process about money by saying, "It's far better to experience warm fuzzies as a parent than cold prickles." The warm fuzzies occur as you watch your thirteen-year-old plan how to stretch his allowance to the end of the month, carefully balancing the price of a decal for his skateboard and the price of a movie. The cold prickles attack when you learn that your twenty-two-year-old son has a $3,000 credit card debt. It's far better to teach the lessons at thirteen when the stakes are lower. This plan grows with your child, and it should save you from the cold prickles.

This system lets you establish a rapport with your children about money. It becomes a subject that is easily discussed rather than one that causes irritation. These are lines of communication that will last and grow.

Good communication is not the only thing the future holds for them. The realism you teach them in this system helps them see what is possible for them; maybe they can't buy the car today, but if they save, there is always tomorrow. They learn the difference between delayed gratification and denial, which helps them feel peaceful while waiting for what they want. They know it's possible. They know it's coming in time.

The habit of saving also contributes to a positive future for your kids. The money they accumulate becomes a tool for opening doors as they enter adulthood. Those successes, in turn, generate more income, which can then be saved and used for future doors. The positive pattern can go on and on. The more their successes build, the more their self-worth and pride in their work are reinforced.

Watching our children grow with their allowance system was rewarding for us and sometimes amusing. In the end, we knew we had done something right when two of our children became accountants; they are now paid to handle other people's money.

Money is not the answer to happiness, but it is an important force in our lives that can create a sense of accomplishment and pride or shame and frustration. I hope that this book and this system will help you give your children control over one more piece in the puzzle that is their lives. If the early habits I encourage can help your kids stride confidently into financial adulthood the way mine did, then I will have fulfilled my greatest wish for this book.

¢ *Sit back and watch them prosper*

CPSIA information can be obtained at www.ICGtesting.com
Printed in the USA
BVOW032356251012

303912BV00001B/3/P